IMAGES OF
BRITAIN

AA

IMAGES OF
BRITAIN

Writers: Ann F. Stonehouse, Charles Phillips
Managing editor: David Popey
Designer: Keith Miller
Cover designer: Tracey Butler
Picture researcher: Paula Boyd-Barrett
Proofreader: Pam Stagg
Image retouching and internal repro: Sarah Montgomery
Production: Rachel Davis

Produced by AA Publishing
© Copyright AA Media Limited 2011

ISBN: 978-0-7495-7200-6 and 978-0-7495-7203-7 (SS)

Published by AA Publishing (a trading name of AA Media Limited, whose registered office is Fanum House, Basing View, Basingstoke RG21 4EA; registered number 06112600).

A04755

The contents of this book are believed correct at the time of printing. Nevertheless, the publishers cannot be held responsible for any errors or omissions or for changes in the details given in this book or for the consequences of any reliance on the information provided by the same. This does not affect your statutory rights.

Editor's note: County and regional boundaries within Britain are subject to change and adjustment. For organizational purposes, the sections of this book are based on the ceremonial counties of England, older Scottish regional boundaries and the Welsh preserved ceremonial county boundaries. The British Crown Dependencies of the Isle of Man and the Channel Islands are listed with the English counties.

Printed in China by C&C Offset Printing Co., Ltd

Visit AA Publishing at theAA.com/shop

Previous pages: The Goring Gap, in Oxfordshire, viewed from Lardon Chase.

Contents

Introduction

Thanks to a network of high-speed motorways, you could drive from one end of Britain to the other in little more than a day. After all, it is about 800 miles (1,300km) from tip to toe. You would gain some fleeting impressions along the way – glittering rivers and lakes, mountain ridges, wide open, empty moorland spaces, rolling farmland, distant villages marked out by church spires and the inevitable sprawling conurbations where the traffic would slow your progress. You might spot some half-familiar landmarks in the passing blur and wonder at the audacity of a sculptor who would create a jumbo-sized angel of rusted iron or the pressure of a prehistoric ice-sheet which could carve out such a diverse landscape. By the time you had glimpsed that snapshot view of a dramatic castle or wandering country footpath, it would be gone, passed in the blink of an eye.

So what's the haste? You could, in reality, spend a lifetime exploring this country of ours and discover something new and surprising each day. This collection of more than 400 superb photographic images has captured some of the best

views of Britain. Explore them in your own time, at your leisure, and enjoy discovering the stories behind some of the most interesting locations across England, Scotland and Wales.

For this is a book for people who are curious about the places around them, who want to see below the surface of a pretty picture. Why is there a temple-like church apparently standing in the middle of a lake? Why was that weird bottle-shaped brick structure built? Where is the Squinty Bridge? Just how old is England's oldest church? What's that new glass building doing in the middle of Manchester? What cargo was that picturesque wreck on the Cornish coast carrying? Why is there an obelisk on that hilltop? Which mountain is that?

Britain has around 19,500 miles (31,400km) of coastline to explore – and you can hardly miss it, when nowhere, even on the mainland, is further than about 70 miles (113km) from the sea. You can contrast the landscapes of salt marsh and sea stack, remote sandy bays and cheerful seaside resorts, cliffs where seabirds nest in their thousands and harbours where fishing boats and sailing craft jostle for space.

Move on then to discover some of the industrial heritage which shaped our landscapes, from coal mining and potteries to woollen textiles and ground-breaking engineering. Contrast the ultra-modern office blocks of our finest cities with venerable mansions and humble cottages, and see the dwellings of the earliest folk to inhabit these islands. Follow the threads of rivers and canals, the history of monarchs and monks, the style of ancient and modern. Take pleasure in the details, identifying some familiar plants and animals. It's a great way to see so much from the comfort of your own armchair.

And of course, you can allow these images to inspire your next day out or holiday. Thanks to our network of national trails, waymarked paths and cycle trails, national parks and heritage sites, Britain is wonderfully accessible to walkers and cyclists. The richness of fascinating historic properties open to public access is remarkable. Perhaps these pages will encourage you to visit somewhere a little different – one of the many islands around the coast, from Wight and Man to Lewis and Orkney, or maybe one of our vibrant cities.

Bottom: Autumnal silver birches in Scotland's Cairngorms National Park are a spectacular reminder that Britain is an island that rewards exploration in all seasons.

Below: A rustic stone barn in the Manifold Valley sets a characteristic Peak District farming scene, on a glorious summer day. Isolated barns like this provide storage out in the fields for winter fodder.

Don't wait for the perfect weather – we British are notorious for our vociferous complaints, and blazing sunshine is rarely the problem. Instead, embrace the changeability of our maritime climate, that gives us the softest of grey days and sparkling snow, as well as clear blue skies and an infinity of cloud patterns. After all, waterfalls show up so much better after a shower of rain.

In an age where you can get a cheap airline flight to just about anywhere in the world it's easy to overlook the beauty and sheer diversity on our doorsteps. This fine collection of photographs is a timely reminder that every corner of Britain has the power to inspire awe and wonder.

Above left: The acid-yellow of oil-seed rape flowers have become a familiar sight across Britain, a relatively modern crop that provides nutrients for the soil as well as seeds crushed for their oil and for fodder.

Left: Loch Katrine is a renowned beauty spot in the Scottish Highlands. Despite its naturalistic appearance, with glorious trees reaching to the shore, the lake is a man-made affair, created to feed clean water to urban populations.

Below: Low tide in Cardiff Bay leaves yachts and small pleasure craft marooned and beached. Britain's coastline is lengthy and varied, and rewards further exploration.

Right: Rolling green slopes around Semer Water, in the Yorkshire Dales, reveals the hand of man in the neatly stacked drystone stone walls. Farming has done much to shape the landscape of Britain.

Overleaf: A dusting of winter snow highlights the beauty of the fells above Ambleside, in the Lake District.

England

Right: The deer at Woburn Abbey lead a pampered life. The 11th Duke of Bedford built up the collection in the mid-19th century, and the 3,000-acre (1,214ha) park now hosts nine species. So successful was the breeding of the rare Pere David deer, that it was saved from extinction and reintroduced to its native China in 1985 by the 14th Duke.

Below: When the enthusiastic amateur architect Thomas, Second Earl de Grey, inherited Wrest Park, near Luton, in 1833, he promptly knocked down the family home and replaced it with a French-style chateau. Extensive gardens were landscaped to include a rococo orangery – the ultimate greenhouse for overwintering tender citrus trees.

Opposite page: The model village of Stewartby was to bricks what Bournville was to chocolate. The town grew up around the London Brick Company works in the 1930s, which favoured the local Oxford clay for its 'fletton' bricks. New owners Hanson PLC built this splendid new headquarters here in 2009, but the parent company has now moved on.

Opposite page: Windsor Castle, England's premier castle – and the Queen's favourite royal residence – dates from 1080, when William I built a stronghold on the one defensible site on the Thames west of London. Remodelled many times, it remains a definitive statement of the wealth and power of the monarchy.

Left: A statue of its founder, Henry VI, stands in front of Eton College. England's most famous public school has educated no less that 19 prime ministers since its humble beginnings in 1441, when it was set up to prepare poor boys for university life at Cambridge.

Below: Non-boaters can enjoy the still waters of the River Thames near Cookham Lock from the Thames Path National Trail.

Right: Bristol's lofty cathedral grew out of an abbey church, battered during the Dissolution, but restored and rebuilt in the mid-19th century by GE Street. This window commemorates the 16th-century abbot John Newland, one of many who contributed to its construction.

Below: Cheerful pastel paintwork adorns the backs of Georgian terraces in Hotwells, Bristol. Set in the fashionable Clifton area, directly north of the city's floating dock, it was once a flourishing spa community with its very own hot spring.

Opposite page: One of Isambard Kingdom Brunel's mighty feats of engineering, the SS *Great Britain*, was floated back to the Western Dock from a watery grave in the Falkland Islands in 1970 and has been lovingly restored to her former glory. Launched from Bristol in 1843, she was the world's first iron-clad steamship.

Overleaf: The Clifton Suspension Bridge spans the rocky gorge of the River Avon above the centre of Bristol. It was the supreme achievement of Isambard Kingdom Brunel, who dreamed up its construction as a young man of 24. It was not completed until after his death, in 1864.

Right: In 1880, the City of London Corporation bought nearly 200 acres (81ha) of ancient common and woodland between Buckingham and Beaconsfield, including extensive beechwoods with 300-year-old trees. Today, Burnham Beeches is preserved as a National Nature Reserve and Site of Special Scientific Interest, the woods are maintained as a public open space.

Below: A statue of John Hampden, Parliamentary hero, stands in Aylesbury's market square. He had been a serving MP for more than 21 years by the time the English Civil War broke out in 1642, and promptly raised a local regiment which became known as the 'Greencoats' to fight off the King's men. Hampden was fatally wounded at the Battle of Chalgrove the following year.

Right: Coombe Hill, at 852ft (260m) is the highest point in the Chiltern Hills, with sweeping views over the Vale of Aylesbury. It is topped by a memorial to local men who died in South Africa during the Second Boer War (1899–1902). Standing some 64ft (20m) tall, it has been the victim of several lightning strikes since its erection in 1904.

Below right: Milton Keynes was developed as a New Town in 1967, and quickly gained a reputation for its innovative modern architecture, its traffic system of seemingly endless roundabouts, and its iconic concrete cows. Today it has grown to a size that has it seeking city status.

Below: A traditionally knotted rope fender protects the bow of a narrowboat on the Thames at Marlow. Narrowboats were the HGVs of their age, often strung together, and pulled by horse-power.

Opposite page: The handsome old market town of Marlow owes its prosperity to the river on which it stands, and is forever associated with the Thameside tales of Izaak Walton *(The Compleat Angler)* and Kenneth Grahame *(The Wind in the Willows)*. Regular flooding meant that the church needed to be completely replaced in the 19th century; its lofty successor receives some protection from the nearby weir.

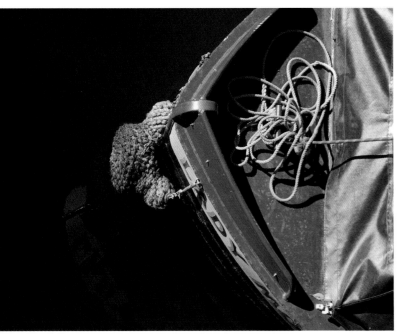

Opposite page: Wicken Fen is England's oldest nature reserve, a wetland habitat that supports around 8,000 plant and animal species. It's a rare survivor of the drainage schemes which turned fen to rich farmland from the 17th century onwards.

Left: The Mathematical Bridge is a favourite on the Cambridge tourist trail. The current structure, built in 1905, replicated earlier designs. William Etheridge, who first built the bridge, was paid £21 for his initial design.

Below: St John's College, part of the University of Cambridge, was established in 1511. It has 11 courtyards – more than any other college – including this, the New Court, added in the 19th century and nicknamed 'the Wedding Cake' for its neo-Gothic stonework.

Below left: Stark rows of white crosses fan out to mark the graves of more than 3,800 US servicemen at the American Military Cemetery in Madingley, near Cambridge. A carved wall of Portland stone records the names of more than 5,000 more, their bodies never recovered, in this unique tribute to Americans who perished while fighting the Allied cause in Europe during the Second World War.

Bottom: Three Gothic arches dwarf the main door in the West Front of Peterborough Cathedral. Their restoration in 2009 included the repair and replacement of 33 weathered 13th-century statues.

Below and opposite page: The octagonal lantern is Ely Cathedral's most famous feature. Richly painted inside, its height of 170 feet (52m) makes it a notable fen landmark for miles around. This glorious building has threatened to sink into the fens on several occasions, but major restoration projects, notably those of George Gilbert Scott in the mid-19th century and the most recent (completed in 2000), have ensured that the 'ship of the fens' will sail on for at least a few centuries more.

Right: The Channel Island archipelago, in the English Channel, offers many interesting sights. Mont Orgueil Castle dominates the headland on Jersey's east coast, overlooking Gorey Harbour. In the mid-15th century the castle was captured by French invaders, but it was soon retaken by the English. In the 17th century it served as the island's prison.

Below: There's been a lighthouse on the northeastern point of the Channel Island of Alderney since 1912, but the last keepers left in 1997. The main beam ceased its 24-hour rotation in 2011, along with the foghorn it had become obsolete in an age of modern computerised navigation systems.

Opposite page: A jumble of fishing boats bob in the waters of Alderney's Braye Harbour, protected by a stone breakwater originally constructed to shelter Royal Navy ships in the 19th century.

Right: The Lovell Radio Telescope at Jodrell Bank Observatory first began exploring the wonders of space in 1957. An impressive 250ft (76m) in diameter, it is the world's third largest fully positional telescope, capable of recording radio waves pulsing from objects galaxies away.

Below: The double herbaceous border is a highlight of the famous gardens at Arley Hall, a Victorian red-brick stately home near Northwich. They are sheltered by a wall on one side and a high topiaried hedge on the opposite side. Recorded on a map of 1848, they are said to be some of the oldest such borders in England.

Opposite page: Perched on a fermentation of wrought iron, the Eastgate Clock is Chester's best-loved landmark. Erected in 1899 to commemorate Queen Victoria's Diamond Jubilee, it stands high above the road on a section of the city's venerable walls.

THIS CLOCK WAS PRESENTED
TO THE CITY BY
EDWARD EVANS-LLOYD
CITIZEN & FREEMAN. 1897

Opposite page: The shattered hull of RMS *Mulheim* lies stranded at Castle Zawn near Land's End, where she ran onto the rocks on a dark March morning in 2003 with her cargo of plastic waste. She is the latest in a long line of Cornish shipwrecks.

Left: The Biomes of the Eden Project, built in a disused clay mine near St Austell, encapsulate environmental gardens from around the world in Cornwall's most successful modern tourist attraction.

Below: The remote Priest's Cove, on Cape Cornwall near St Just, provides just enough rocky shore for broad-beamed local fishing boats to haul clear of the sea.

Right: Manacle Point and the reef of jagged rocks beyond form some of the most treacherous coastline for sailors, on this windswept southwestern tip of England. The Manacles owe their name, not to their grip on the seafaring community, but rather to the Cornish for 'church rocks', *maen-eglos.*

Below: Sea-cut stacks and golden sands characterize Gwithian Beach, at the eastern tip of St Ives Bay. It's a popular spot for surfers, when the wind and tide are right. Godrevy Lighthouse beams out from the distant offshore island.

Opposite page, left: Tiny ferns and mosses relish the damp crevices of Cumbria's drystone walls.

Opposite page, right: The ancient walls of Lanercost Priory, founded by Robert de Veaux in 1169 to house Augustinian Canons, reveal red sandstone blocks taken from the Roman structure of Hadrian's Wall, close by.

Right: Sheep are the mainstay of farming in the high fells of Cumbria. Hardy breeds such as the local grey Herdwick will stay in the hills year-round, while others will over-winter in the lower valleys.

Below: Bassenthwaite Lake reflects the western flanks of Skiddaw. Some 4 miles (6km) long, this is the only lake in the Lake District to carry 'lake' in its name; others are more commonly named 'water'.

Right: A dusting of snow adorns the peaks of Cat Bells and Dale Head, viewed across tranquil Derwent Water.

Below: Castlerigg Stone Circle, above Keswick, is a late neolithic site, probably erected around 3000BC for ceremonial purposes. Thirty-eight boulders surround a rectangle, formed by another ten stones.

Opposite page: The valley of Great Langdale sweeps down from the rocky pinnacles of the Langdale Pikes. These include the wonderfully named Pike of Stickle and Pavey Ark. Harrison Stickle, at 2,415ft (736m), is the highest in this range.

Overleaf: Resembling an upturned keel, the fell of Yewbarrow looms over Wast Water, in the western Lake District.

Opposite page: The Peak District National Park covers some 555 square miles (1,438sq km), and was Britain's first National Park, established in 1951. This view of Dovedale, taken from Thorpe Cloud, shows Bunster Hill and the River Dove flowing in the wooded ravine below. The river itself flows for 45 miles (72.4km), but only the section between Milldale and Bunster Hill is known as Dovedale.

Left: A bumble bee forages for nectar on a flower of black knapweed. This summer wild flower is commonly found in open grassland in the area, and is also known as hardheads or lesser knapweed.

Below: Matlock Bath, clinging to a steep-sided gorge on the River Derwent, grew up as a spa resort in the 19th century. Its healing wells had been popular since the end of the 17th century. Today this charming town is still a favourite with visitors to the Peak District.

Right: The rugged gritstone ridge of Curbar Edge, in the eastern area of the national park, is littered with ancient remains including a stone circle at Froggatt Edge, and a Bronze Age burial cist or cairn.

Below: Camouflaged in the gritstone, on the plateau of Kinder Scout, a young mountain hare eyes passers by. It was a mass trespass on this mountain in 1932, protesting at the lack of access for walkers, that eventually helped to establish a right to roam in open country.

Opposite page, right: Smart iron railings decorate the Victorian bandstand in the Pavilion Gardens in the spa town of Buxton. Set in 23 acres (9ha) of landscaped municipal park, this pleasure garden was laid out by Edward Milner in 1871, and is now a popular venue for weddings.

Opposite page, left: A dizzying cable car ride offers superb views over the limestone gorge near Matlock Bath. The cabs carry visitors up the hillside known as the Heights of Abraham, which is riddled with limestone caves such as the Great Masson Cavern and the Great Rutland Cavern-Nestus Mine.

Below: Ladybower Reservoir, in Derbyshire's Upper Derwent Valley finally opened in 1945, after its construction was interrupted by the war. Two villages were drowned in the process. Today, it provides clean drinking water for the people of Derby, Leicester and Sheffield.

Right: Farmers and tin miners used what are known as clapper bridges to negotiate Dartmoor's main rivers. They often consisted of little more than stone slabs laid across stepping stones. This more sophisticated structure, built to allow for flooding, dates from the 13th century and crosses the River Dart at Postbridge, in Devon.

Below: Nobody is quite sure who Bowerman was, or whether this is a fair representation of his profile, but he has given his name to an extraordinary weathered granite outcrop on Hayne Down, near the Dartmoor village of Manaton: Bowerman's Nose.

Right: Carpets of bluebells are a familiar sight in parts of Devon, seen at their best in late April and May, and are often an indicator of ancient woodland.

Below: The sturdy remains of the engine house from the Wheal Betsy mine on Dartmoor. Tin mining was established in the area before Roman times, and such structures were once, a common sight.

Opposite page: Lynmouth is a picturesque harbour village located on the north coast of Exmoor, at the foot of cliffs so steep that the area is nicknamed 'Little Switzerland'. A cable railway, opened in 1890 and uniquely powered by a combination of water balance and gravity, hauls visitors up to the sister village of Lynton.

Opposite page: A spectacular landslide at Mupe Bay, near Lulworth, reveals the pristine chalk that characterizes the Dorset Heritage Coast. Signs of a fossil forest have been uncovered here, dating to the Jurassic period.

Left: The abbey church at Sherborne, built in golden Ham stone, is famed for its fan vaulting, which dates from around 1490. Two kings of Wessex were buried on this spot in the 9th century. Today, a dedicated choir of men and boys, the youngest aged just eight, regularly fill this glorious nave with song.

Below: Portland stone, a fine-textured, greyish oolitic limestone, has been taken from this little island since Roman times and transported around the world. It dresses the facades of many of London's finest buildings, including St Paul's Cathedral. The *Spirit of Portland* statue by Joanna Szuwalska overlooks the town of Portland and depicts a stonemason on one side and a fisherman on the other.

Left: The planispiral of an ammonite shell, preserved in the stone. Larger fossils of these ancient, long-extinct sea creatures are frequently seen as decorations built into the walls of Dorset cottages.

Below: The huge and toothy ruin of Corfe Castle seems to fill the gap in the wall of the Purbeck Hills with its presence. Set on a high mound, it must have been massively imposing when whole. The Norman keep dates from around 1106, and bears a gory history of murder and imprisonment.

Opposite page: Durdle Door is a natural stone arch on the Dorset shore, set on a naturally curving bay that is popular with holidaymakers. It's a familiar landmark on the South West Coast Path, Britain's longest national trail which extends for 630 miles (1,014km) from Minehead in Somerset all the way to Poole in Dorset.

Right: England's most spectacularly placed cathedral crowns a great rocky peninsula in a horseshoe bend of the River Wear. Containing the shrine of St Cuthbert, the massive Norman church at Durham was begun in 1039 and, remarkably, took only around 40 years to construct. Three thousand Scots were imprisoned in the cathedral by Oliver Cromwell's men during the Civil War.

Below: Langdon Beck is a sprawling rural community in Teesdale, County Durham, in the shadow of the rolling Northern Pennine hills. The famous Pennine Way long distance footpath passes through here on its way to Kirk Yetholm in the Scottish Borders.

Opposite page: St Mary the Virgin, Saffron Walden, is the biggest parish church in Essex, and was built around 1430 under the guidance of John Wastell – better known as the chief mason of King's College Chapel in Cambridge. The town takes its name from the growing of the precious saffron crocus here in the 16th and 17th centuries.

Left: Farmer John Webb built his windmill in Thaxted in 1804, from bricks manufactured just a couple of miles away. It successfully ground the local grain for a century, before falling into disuse. In recent years it has undergone major restoration.

Below: Greensted Church, just outside the Essex town of Chipping Ongar, is quite simply the oldest wooden church in the world. It dates back at least as far as the 7th century, although timbers have been replaced and adjustments made to the structure over the years. The weatherboarded bell tower may have been a medieval addition.

Right: The curious astronomical clock in Gloucester Cathedral by Henry Wilson was placed there in memory of the 19th-century mathematician Bartholomew Price. Price is remembered as the teacher of Lewis Carroll, who used his old tutor's nickname, 'the Bat,' in his doggerel rhyme for *Alice in Wonderland*, 'Twinkle, twinkle, little bat.'

Below: The delicate fan vaulting in the cloister of Gloucester Cathedral is among the oldest in the country, and it is possible that fan vaulting was invented here when the church was rebuilt in the 14th century. It was then the abbey church of the Benedictine monastery of St Peter.

Left and below: Westonbirt Arboretum, near Tetbury in Gloucestershire, is home to around 16,000 trees from temperate countries all around the world, including Japan, China and North and South America. The collection, started in 1829, is of national importance, and can be readily accessed by all. Favourite times to visit are autumn, for the leaf colour (the maples show fabulous shades of scarlet), and spring for the flowering rhododendrons and azaleas.

Right: Neatly clipped yew trees are a feature of Painswick's churchyard. The clock on the venerable 11th-century tower of St Mary's Church was restored in 2001.

Below: Houses of golden stone line Blockley's High Street. This peaceful, quintessential Cotswold village was once a hive of industry, shifting from the manufacture of woollen cloth to the spinning and weaving of fine silk for ribbons in the 18th century.

Opposite page: A distant view of Winchcombe, a typically quaint Cotswold town set in gently rolling farmland. Saxons first settled here, and its location at the crossing of ways is still evident today from the number of footpaths and national trails that pass through the town.

Opposite page, left: Purple bell heather grows extensively on the open heathland of the New Forest, an area of land first preserved by William I as a royal hunting ground in the 11th century, and now at the heart of the New Forest National Park.

Below: HMS *Victory*, the veteran of five sea battles, is the only great wooden battleship to be completely preserved, and is part of the Royal Navy's historic collection in Portsmouth. It was built in 1765, and played a starring role in the Battle of Trafalgar (1805) as Admiral Lord Nelson's flagship. The spot where that heroic leader died is still proudly pointed out by the town's guides.

Opposite page, right: Taller than the London Eye, Portsmouth's Spinnaker Tower was completed in 2005, a 558ft (170m) symbol of civic pride growing out of the modern harbourside shopping centre of Gunwharf Quays. Designed to evoke a ship's mast, it gives extensive views along the coast and over the Isle of Wight.

Overleaf: Visitors to the New Forest expecting a landscape of endless woodland are swiftly disillusioned. Rolling Rockford Common is more typical of the area, and offers grazing for ponies, cattle and pigs, and habitat for a variety of wildlife including birds such as the Dartford Warbler, snakes and rare sand lizards.

Below left: The Domesday Book provided the first record of a castle on this rocky spur above the River Wye, built by Godric Mapplestone to guard the river crossing. The hefty ruins of Goodrich Castle seen today are the remains of a 15th-century structure, the former residence of the Earls of Shrewsbury.

Below: Threaded by the River Dore and flanked by rich pastures, the Golden Valley is a beauty spot lying to the south of Vowchurch.

Opposite page: The small Norman cathedral of Hereford, with its forest of pink sandstone columns lining the nave, is one of the finest in England. The massive central tower of around 1325 adds distinction to every view of the building. The cathedral's most remarkable treasure is the Mappa Mundi, a 13th-century map of the world, one of the earliest in existence.

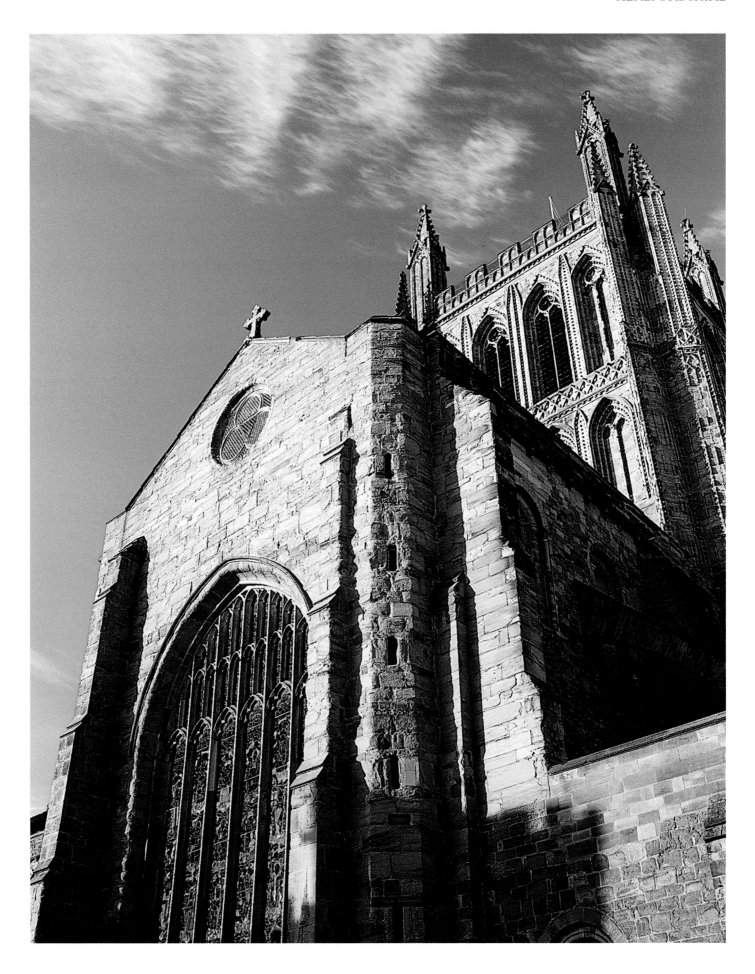

Left: The Grand Union Canal links London with Birmingham, and was only finally completed in 1929 – although certain sections are much older than that, of course. Land-locked Hertfordshire gained a 'port' at Berkhamsted, which is now used by pleasure craft rather than freight.

Below: The canalside in Berkhamsted is an unexpected place to find a genuine First Nations totem pole. It was carved from red cedar in Vancouver Island, Canada, and erected in 1968 in a now private garden, in memory of a local man who was saved from starvation there by members of the local Kwakiutl tribe, in the 19th century.

Above: A shady section on the circular 166-mile (267km) walking route known as the Hertfordshire Way, near Much Hadham. Coaches on their way from London to Cambridge used to stop at the inn here to change horses, but now the village is a peaceful backwater.

Right: St Albans Cathedral was built on the hilltop above the River Ver where Britain's first Christian martyr, Alban, was beheaded in the third century. The abbey subsequently founded here in his memory became one of the richest in England. The abbey church (not a cathedral until 1877) was constructed partly of Roman bricks from the city of Verulamium. The ornate Wallingford Screen dates to 1480.

Right: The fortress of Peel Castle, on the British Crown Dependency of the Isle of Man, stands on St Patrick's Island and is linked to Peel by a causeway. The Vikings were the first to spot the defensive potential of the site in the 11th century, rebuilding in the local red sandstone some 300 years later. The shell of the Cathedral of St German stands within the walls.

Below: The monster wheel called Lady Isabella, used to drain a lead mine at Laxey, is 72.5ft (22m) in diameter. Churning 168 buckets, it is the largest surviving waterwheel in the British Isles, and first operated in 1854.

Opposite page: Early settlers on the Isle of Man left clues to their beliefs in the form of burial mounds. The Cashtal-yn-Ard burial chamber, one of three identified hereabouts, is believed to have held the bodies of five Neolithic chieftains and their families.

Opposite page: The Solent – the body of water between Southampton and the Isle of Wight – attracts thousands of yachts and other small craft and is the training ground of Olympic champions. The Round-the-Island Race in June is a highlight of the sailing calendar. Here a sailor hoists his sail in Cowes Harbour.

Below: Built at the mouth of the River Medina, Cowes is a crowded little harbour that takes a particular cachet from its location as the headquarters of the Royal Yacht Squadron, the most prestigious sailing club in the world. Its members roll has included the explorer Robert Falcon Scott, prime minister Edward Heath and the Duke of Edinburgh.

Right: A restored Gothic arch on the church at Newport, principal town on the island. The church is dedicated to two St Thomases, and is the burial place of Elizabeth, the tragic young daughter of Charles I, who died here in 1650.

Below: Alfred, Lord Tennyson, poet of the Victorian age, loved the Isle of Wight and made his home at Farringdon House, Freshwater, hoping to escape the pressures of his eager fans on the mainland. He lived there for 40 years, and this monument was raised in his honour on the nearby down in 1897.

Opposite page: The line of chalk which runs through the Isle of Wight emerges in the west in the spectacular chalk stacks of the Needles. The windswept lighthouse at their tip, topped by a helipad, was manned until 1994.

Previous pages: Stately statues and gargoyles adorn the exterior of Canterbury Cathedral, which became a major destination for pilgrims after the murder there of Thomas à Becket in 1178, on the instructions of Henry II.

Right: Kent is famous for its oysters, and Whitstable's oyster bar has been going strong since 1856, winning just about every award going in recent years.

Below: Gaily painted seaside beach huts are a British phenomenon linked to our history of bucket-and-spade holidays and our nostalgia for sand sandwiches and dripping ice creams eaten in a chill wind. These little havens occupy the shore at Whitstable.

Opposite page: Chalk stacks and soft golden sands characterize Botany Bay, the most northerly of the seven bays of Broadstairs. Shallow waters and a reef of rock pools make this popular with families in summer.

Opposite page: Blackpool boasts no fewer than three piers, each vying to attract the most visitors. The Central Pier has a theatre for live music shows, a fun fair, and a Ferris wheel, 108ft high (32m), which gives great panoramic views along the coast.

Right: Sticky pink peppermint-flavoured rock is the ultimate holiday souvenir, and inserting the letters is a skill all of its own, a practice still performed by hand.

Below: Donkeys wait patiently to offer children rides on the beach at Blackpool, as they have done since 1890. In modern times the donkeys' working week is strictly monitored, with no more than 48 hours of actual labour permitted, and Friday a compulsory day of rest.

Right: A quartet of rivers pours down from the uplands of the Forest of Bowland: the Ribble, the Hodder, the Wyre and the Lune. In their lower stretches, pockets of ancient forest have been preserved, a haven for colonies of pipistrelle and Daubenton's bats.

Below: The Ashton Memorial is a well-loved Lancaster landmark, located in leafy Williamson Park. It was constructed in 1909 by Lord Ashton, the city's 'lino king', as a memorial to his second wife Jessy. There are fabulous views over Morecambe Bay from the exterior gallery, and the interior chamber is used for concerts and weddings.

Right: A robin perches on a canalside post at Foxton's staircase locks. Notoriously territorial little birds, they live year-round in the UK, their numbers boosted by migrants from Europe in winter.

Below: The splendid mansion of Belvoir (pronounced 'beaver') Castle is home to the Duke of Rutland, and has appeared in many a movie, including *The Da Vinci Code* (2006), where it doubled as the Pope's palace.

Opposite page: Views over Leicestershire's Bradgate Country Park – a former medieval deer park.

Right: Spalding in Lincolnshire is a centre for bulb growing, and in spring its fertile flatlands are transformed into a colourful carpet of tulips and daffodils.

Below: Sandy dunes line the Lincolnshire coast between Mablethorpe and Saltfleet. Coarse marram grass is planted to hold the sand down in the teeth of the North Sea gales.

Opposite page, top and bottom: Mellow local sandstone dignifies the handsome old municipal buildings of Stamford, a town that grew in the 17th and 18th centuries thanks to its location on the Great North Road, the main travel link between London and York.

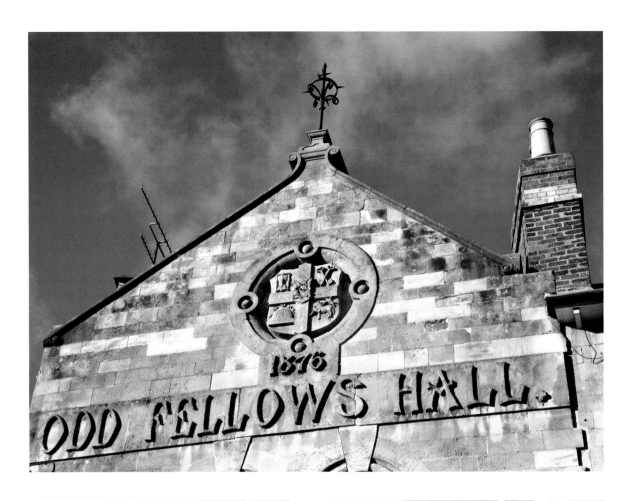

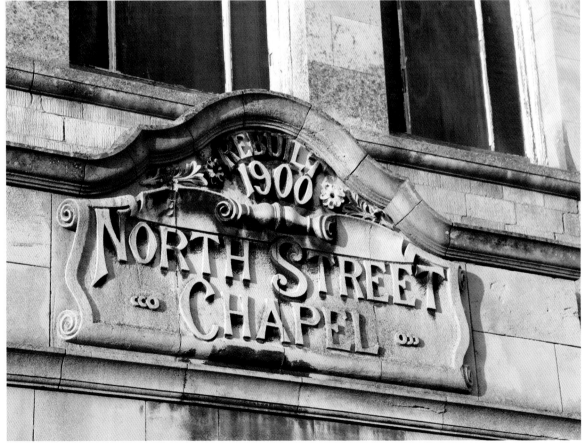

Left: The London Eye was proposed as a temporary structure to celebrate the Millennium. However, it has proved such a success – more than 10,000 people daily step into a capsule for the half-hour circuit – that it is likely to remain part of the London skyline for many years to come.

Below: A Grecian frieze encircles the Royal Albert Hall, in the heart of Kensington, which was designed in the 19th century as a multi-purpose centre to promote understanding and enjoyment of the arts and sciences. Today it hosts a variety of events, from boxing matches to the famous Promenade concerts.

Above: A geometrically patterned skin of glass marks the curvaceous structure of 30 St Mary Axe – an office complex better known as the Gherkin. With it, architect Norman Foster changed the London skyline for ever, and opened the doors to more dramatic structures such as the Shard.

Right: Architect Richard Rogers designed a building for Lloyds of London that was effectively inside out. With its functions visible on the outside, the interior can remain light, spacious and comparatively uncluttered.

Below: Dress uniform and bearskin caps are the order of the day for the ceremonial Changing of the Guard outside Buckingham Palace. Five different regiments of the British Army take turns to supply the Queen's footguard: their collar badges reveal these as members of the Scots Guards.

Opposite page: Tower Bridge, London's iconic gateway on the River Thames since 1894, is both a swing and bascule bridge that is lifted around 1,000 times a year. Horizontal walkways 143ft (44m) above the river brace and join the two towers.

Opposite page: The Victoria Memorial, which now stands on a busy traffic island in front of Buckingham Palace, at the top of the Mall, was erected by Edward VII in tribute to his late mother. The gilded, winged figure on the top represents Victory.

Left: The fountains in Trafalgar Square, designed by Sir Edward Lutyens in the early 20th century, fill shallow pools that provide cool relief on hot summer days in the capital.

Below: The gracious sunken garden at Kensington Palace was designed along calm, classical lines in 1908 and offers a tranquil oasis – for moorhens and other visitors.

Right: London's parks offer a refreshing escape for office workers and tourists alike on sunny days in the city. This is Green Park, which lies behind Buckingham Palace.

Below right: Fairy lights illuminate the delicate iron tracery of the Albert Bridge, which crosses the Thames by Chelsea.

Below: The Golden Jubilee footbridges, opened in 2003, are the newest river crossings in central London. They run either side of the sturdy Hungerford rail bridge of 1859, to link the South Bank and Waterloo with the Victoria Embankment.

Opposite page: The great dome of St Paul's Cathedral looms at the northern end of the Millennium Footbridge. London's most sizeable landmark for many years, it survived the Blitz bombing of the Second World War remarkably unscathed.

Right: Redevelopment of the old Salford Docks, at the end of the Manchester Ship Canal, included the construction of this elegant Millennium Bridge in 2000. Hydraulics allow it to lift for the occasional passing vessel; otherwise, it is a key pedestrian route into the shiny new Salford Quays complex, with the Lowry, a temple to the performing and visual arts, at its heart.

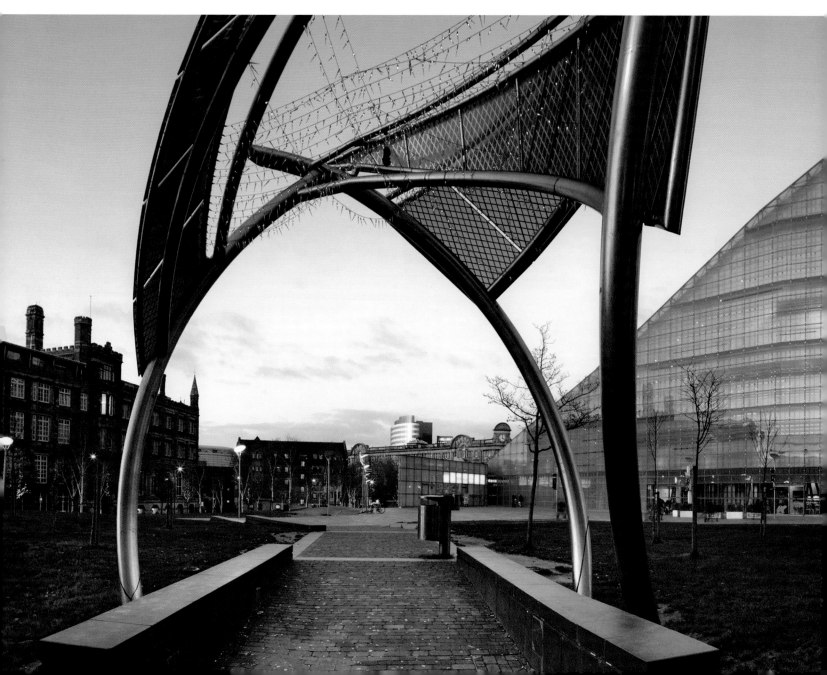

Left: The Rochdale Canal linked up to the older Bridgewater Canal at Castlefield, Manchester, in 1805, and the area developed into a busy junction of railways and waterways in the years that followed. This rich history is celebrated in the Urban Heritage Park, the first of its kind in the UK.

Below: The aftermath of the IRA bomb that ripped through the centre of Manchester in 1996, allowed for imaginative regeneration projects, including the glass Urbis building in Cathedral Gardens. Completed in 2002, it held various exhibitions and collections before settling down as the new home of the National Football Museum in 2011.

Opposite page: Liverpool's magnificent Royal Liver Building, standing proud on the waterside by the redeveloped Albert Dock, is topped by the 'Liver Birds' – two bronze mythical birds that have come to symbolize the city.

Right: Liverpool's Catholic Metropolitan Cathedral of Christ the King is a striking piece of modernist architecture designed by Frederick Gibberd and completed in 1967. The circular interior is bathed in coloured light from the stained glass that surrounds the central tower.

Left: Broadleaf planting along the roadside in Thetford Forest helps to break up the monotony of Scots pines. The woodland, studded with open sandy heath, is a key feature of the dry Breckland area to the west of Norwich.

Below: Norwich's castle is unmistakably Norman in design, standing on a raised earthwork, or motte. The neat stonework is in fact the product of an exterior makeover by Anthony Salvin in 1824, which replicated the original blank arcading. Today the sturdy keep holds the city's excellent museum and collection of paintings by the Norwich School of Artists.

Left: There's been a settlement at Weybourne on the Norfolk coast since the Domesday survey noted a handful of houses at 'Wabrunna', and it's a pretty safe bet that folk were fishing from the shore in those times, too. Bass and mackerel are favourite summer catches.

Below: Comparatively peaceful in summertime, the windswept beach at Horsey Gap is taken over by grey seals in winter. Between December and February these sleek, blubberous sea mammals come ashore to give birth to silvery-white pups. The pups are weaned after just three weeks, so must gain independence quickly.

Opposite page, left: Bishop Herbert de Losinga built Norwich Cathedral in about 1100. Its Gothic spire, 315 feet (96m) high, was added by Bishop Goldwell after a fire destroyed the original in 1463.

Opposite page, far right: The sheltered channels of the Norfolk Broads make them the perfect destination for messing about in boats.

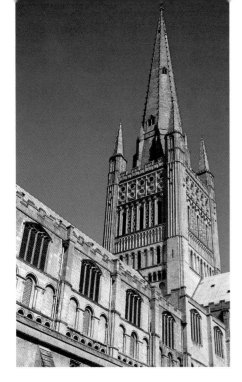

Right: An aerial view shows the triangular form of Rushton Lodge, near Kettering, a puzzle of a building constructed by the eccentric Sir Thomas Tresham in the 1590s as a proclamation of his Roman Catholic faith. It is a folly devoted to the Holy Trinity and number three, with three floors, three triangular gables on each side, and even trefoil windows.

Below: The stained glass in the windows of St Mary Magdalene, in the village of Geddington, is Victorian. The church, however, dates back to the end of the first century, and has an unexpected history of royal patronage, thanks to its proximity to a royal hunting lodge frequented by medieval kings.

Opposite page: The buildings of Oundle School are scattered throughout the ancient market town, giving its pupils a unique place in the local community. It was founded in 1556 as a grammar school by William Laxton, Lord Mayor of London. This is the gable of the Great Hall, built in 1908 for assemblies and concerts.

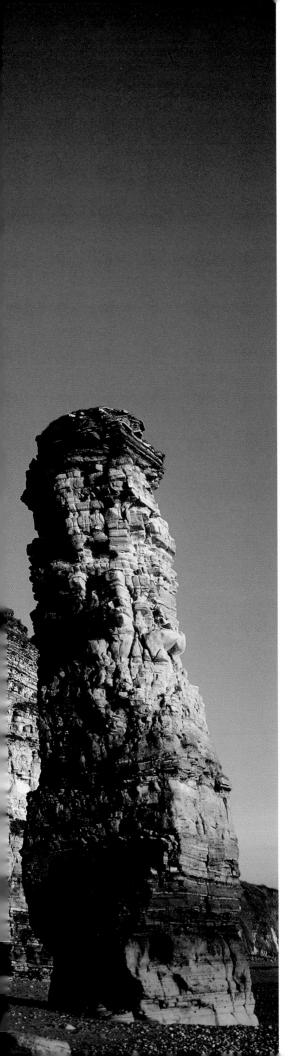

Left: Fanciful names have been given to the extraordinary formations in the weathered limestone cliffs at Marsden Bay, in South Shields. This is Lot's Wife, named after the figure in the Bible who was turned to a pillar of salt. The strata in these cliffs provide good nesting sites for kittiwakes and a variety of other seabirds.

Below: The coastal village of Alnmouth developed as a centre of boatbuilding, trade and smuggling in the early 13th century. In 1806, a violent storm reshaped the entrance to the estuary and swept away the hill where the church stood – today a wooden cross marks the spot.

Right: Yeavering Bell, in the Cheviot Hills, is a 1,182ft (360m) summit with superb views. Small wonder then, that a massive fort was built here during the Iron Age, numbering more than 130 timber buildings.

Opposite page, top: The Farne Islands, a rocky archipelago off the Northumberland coast near Seahouses, provide a summer breeding ground for puffins. These endearing seabirds nest in burrows dug out of the soft topsoil.

Opposite page, centre: Roman emperor Hadrian boldly decreed that a wall should be built across the top of Northumberland in AD122, to keep out the marauding Picts of the north. Much of it still exists, and its 73-mile (117km) route can be followed from coast to coast on a modern footpath, or national trail. Here the wall marches straight over the top of Housesteads Crag.

Opposite page, bottom: Grace Darling was a humble lighthouse keeper's daughter who shot to celebrity status in 1838 when, at the age of 23, she rowed out in high seas to save the passengers and crew of the wrecked SS *Forfarshire*. On her untimely death of tuberculosis just four years later, she was buried in Bamburgh, and an elaborate memorial was raised in the churchyard.

Far left: Newstead Abbey was the ancestral home of Lord Byron, the poet who became famous for his romantic excess and general dissipation. He found the crumbling house, with its medieval cloisters and vast parkland, a money pit, and was relieved to sell it on in 1818. In the grounds there is a touching memorial to his dog, Boatswain, who died of rabies in 1808; Byron hoped to be buried beside him on his death in 1824, but ended up at nearby Hucknell Torkard instead.

Left: Farmland around the village of West Leake, with a ripening crop of oil seed rape. A distant member of the turnip family, the crop is grown for its oil, and as a soil-improver on cereal farms.

Below: The East Coast Main Line railway races through Nottinghamshire on its way between London and Edinburgh. Around the halfway point, south of Retford, it passes beside the disused gravel pits which now form the Daneshill Lakes Nature Reserve, which provide a wetland habitat for butterflies, warblers and other wildlife.

Bottom: The power station at Ratcliffe on Soar burns coal to produce electricity for around two million homes. Its cooling towers are clearly visible from the M1, northeast of Kegworth.

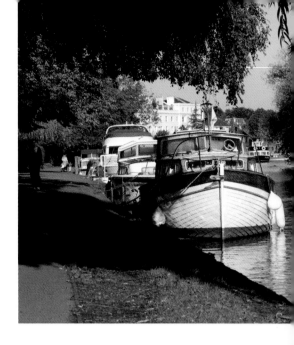

Right: Stately Henley-on-Thames takes its name from the river which runs through it. On the first weekend in July the town devotes itself to the fun of the annual regatta, first held in 1839, with rowing races held over five champagne-fuelled days.

Below: Rhime-frosted watermeadows lie beside the River Windrush below Burford. This idyllic Cotswold town, to the west of Oxford, grew up around the lucrative wool trade of the 14th to 17th centuries.

Opposite page: John Churchill, first Duke of Marlborough, bought a chunk of Woodstock's former royal hunting ground to build his mansion in 1705, helped by a hefty grant from Queen Anne in gratitude for thrashing the French army in the previous year. 'Capability' Brown later remodelled the park at Blenheim, but the Great Bridge is by the house's original designer, Thomas Vanbrugh.

Left: Merton, founded in 1264 is one of the 38 colleges that make up the University of Oxford, and boasts JRR Tolkien and TS Eliot among its eminent past associates – one as a professor, the other a student. The college is set on the edge of the pleasant parkland known as Christ Church Meadows.

Below left: Oxford's prestigious New College was founded in 1379 by William Wykeham, the Bishop of Winchester, and had strong links with Winchester College school from the start, including a shared master builder in William Wynford.

Below: In a city centre laid out long before cars became the local industry, bicycles are the vehicles of choice for most Oxford students and residents.

Opposite page: Built in the 18th century to house a library of scientific tomes, the Radcliffe Camera is one of Oxford University's most distinctive buildings. John Radcliffe, after whom it is named, was royal physician to William and Mary, and the rotunda reflects the Palladian style that was the height of fashion at that time.

Above: The reservoir of Rutland Water offers a variety of activities, including trout and coarse fishing. There's a sailing club, and a little launch, the *Rutland Belle*, which ferries passengers around.

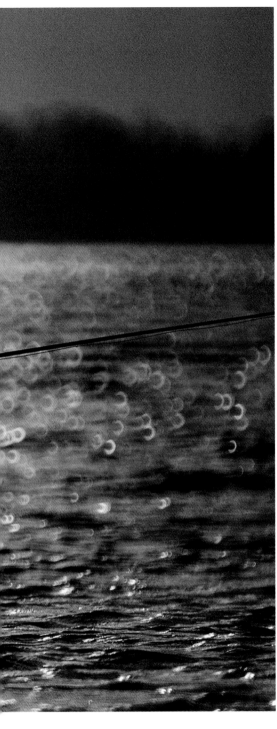

Right: When Anglian Water flooded the twin valleys of the River Gwash in 1975 to build a reservoir, they drowned two villages along the way. They were determined, however, to preserve handsome St Matthews Church, the private chapel, on the former Normanton Estate. Accordingly, a protective bank was built around the church and it is now a museum, accessed via a causeway.

Below: A wild pony grazes the high moorland of the Long Mynd, a section of the Shropshire Hills that is now preserved by the National Trust. Lying roughly north to south, it stretches for about 7 miles (11km) and is littered with prehistoric remains.

Opposite page: The Wrekin is a Shropshire landmark that sticks up 1,335ft (407m) from the plain to the west of Telford. It is topped by the much loved feature of the Wrekin Beacon, a flashing red light on the TV transmission mast that was introduced at the millennium and serves no practical purpose.

Opposite: A bottle-shaped kiln marks the site of a former porcelain works, now the Coalport China Museum and part of the Ironbridge Gorge heritage park. Fine bone china was manufactured here between 1795 and 1926, in a factory started by John Rose.

Above: The Iron Bridge, over the Severn, gave its name to this Shropshire gorge, and is a potent symbol of the Industrial Revolution that transformed manufacturing in Britain in the 18th and 19th centuries. Constructed by Abraham Darby in 1779, it was the first all-iron bridge in the world, and today it is heralded as an innovation that well deserves its World Heritage Site status.

Left and below: The mound of Glastonbury Tor in Somerset is crowned by a lonely stone tower – all that remains of the 14th-century Chapel of St Michael, dismantled for its stones. This is believed to be a sacred place of great antiquity, and the contour lines on the side of the hill may mark the route of a winding spiral path up to the summit, used in pagan rituals long before the coming of Christianity. Some say it is the home of the mysterious and mythical King of the Fairies.

Right: The essence of classical Georgian style and elegance is epitomized by the Royal Crescent in Bath. It was designed by John Wood the Younger and constructed between 1767 and 1774, helping to make Bath the most fashionable of spa towns.

Below: A stone arch frames a cobbled lane off Trim Street in the heart of Bath. James Wolfe, hero of the battle for Quebec in 1759, was a resident of Trim Street, a road of shops and houses that was built around 1707.

Opposite page: A city for all ages: medieval Bath Abbey rises behind the Roman Great Bath, today overlooked by the windows of the Georgian Pump Room. Jane Austen, who lived in Bath from 1801 to 1806, set two of her novels here: *Northanger Abbey* and *Persuasion*.

Left and below: North Cadbury is a village in the southeast corner of the county of Somerset, with a history that dates back to the Norman Conquest. Its large Church of St Michael the Archangel, pictured here, dates from 1417, although the tower is believed to be older. The church is associated with the Botreaux family, who in 1423 converted it into a college, with seven chaplains and four clerks. The interior was greatly restored in the 1980s.

Opposite page: The gritstone escarpments of the Roaches and Hen Cloud lie in the southwest of the Peak District National Park, and form a popular practice ground for climbers as well as walkers. The area has been associated with a colony of wallabies, naturalized after their escape from a private zoo.

Below: The Gladstone Pottery Museum at Longton is a Victorian time capsule, with displays of decorative ceramic tiles, toilet bowls and other functional stoneware alongside more decorative pieces. The evocative bottle-shaped chimneys, once a familiar sight across Stoke-on-Trent, were the kilns where the pottery was fired.

Left: Looking out from the gaping mouth of Thor's Cave, in the side of a crag high above the River Manifold, near Wetton. The cave was inhabited in prehistoric times and during the Celtic, Roman and Anglo-Saxon periods. From the outside the entrance looks like a railway arch – though it is, in fact, entirely natural.

Below and opposite page: Lichfield Cathedral is distinguished by its three spires, known as 'the Ladies of the Vale'. It was constructed of the local reddish sandstone in medieval times, and is home to the eighth-century illuminated manuscript, the Lichfield Gospels. Another treasure is the Lichfield Angel, a vivid medieval relief carving discovered during archaeological work within the building in 2003. Stone figures on the West Front of the cathedral (below) were restored by George Gilbert Scott in the 19th century.

Far left: Lobsters are the catch of the day at Aldeburgh, a venerable town on the Suffolk coast linked to its most famous former resident, the 20th-century composer Benjamin Britten.

Left: Hiring a boat and rowing on the River Stour at Dedham is one of the nicest possible ways to explore 'Constable Country' – the landscapes familiar from the paintings of John Constable, born in nearby East Bergholt in 1776. Alfred Munnings is the other artist celebrated in the village – famous for his horse paintings, he lived just up the hill from here, until his death in 1959.

Below: The marshes of Blythburgh lie inland from the coast at Southwold, where the River Blyth flows into the sea. Blythburgh Water is actually a lagoon, created after the devastating floods of 1953, when much of the East Anglian coast was innundated. Mud-loving waders including avocets may be seen here, and bitterns may be heard in the reedbeds.

Right: Painted beach huts line the shore defences at Southwold. The town was bombarded by a German naval force during the First World War because of the perceived threat from its 18th-century cannons, which faced out over the sea. Long-obsolete, they had been captured from the Jacobites by the Duke of Cumberland in 1745.

Below: The splendid keep at Orford was built by Henry II in the 12th century as a display of royal power, to impress the natives in general and the dissenting local bigwigs, the Bigod family, in particular. Still inhabited in the 19th century, it found a new use during the Second World War as a radar station.

Right: Leith Hill tower is an 18th-century observation point, giving magnificent views over the rolling countryside of Surrey. The folly was built by Richard Hull, who insisted on being buried underneath it on his death in 1772. The hill itself is the highest point on the Greensand Ridge, an escarpment, which gives its name to the 108-mile (174km) Greensand Way footpath, leading all the way to Kent.

Below: An heraldic lion guards the entrance to Hampton Court, the extensive Thames-side palace built for Cardinal Wolsey and taken over by Henry VIII in 1529.

Left: In 2004 Wisley launched its own variety of clematis on the world – named 'Wisley' in honour of the garden's bicentennial celebrations.

Below: Wisley describes itself as the flagship garden of the Royal Horticultural Society, and it certainly never fails to impress, attracting almost a million visitors each year. It covers around 240 acres (97ha), and includes the vast new Bicentenary Glasshouse. Opened in 2007, this showcases plants from desert, tropical and temperate climates around the world.

Opposite page and this page: The rolling chalk hills of the South Downs were incorporated into Britain's newest National Park in 2011. Arable farming gives way to grassland on the slopes, grazed by rabbits and sheep, and the area is studded with pretty flint villages and ancient farmhouses. These images were taken around Ditchling (right and opposite) and Alfriston (below). To the south, the chalk is exposed along the famous white cliffs of southern England.

Left: The charming old Mermaid Inn at Rye is a veritable institution, with the current building dating from 1420, and riddled with tales of smugglers and seadogs. Set at the top of a narrow lane, which leads down to the old harbour, it has numbered royalty and celebrities among its guests over the centuries, appropriately including Hollywood actor and pirate-impersonator Johnny Depp.

Below: Tall wooden sheds on the beach at Hastings are used by local fishermen to dry and store their nets. When not in use, their boats are hauled up onto the shingle beach, known as the Stade.

Opposite page: The white chalk bastion of Beachy Head, near Eastbourne, commands superb views along the Channel coast, towards the Isle of Wight in one direction and Romney Marsh in the other. The red-and-white lighthouse at its foot was built in 1902.

Opposite page: Canopied balconies recall the Regency age in the elegant terrace houses of Regency Square, Brighton. The Prince Regent (later George IV) left his own particular stamp on the town in the form of the Moghul-style Brighton Pavilion.

Left: Brighton's broad Promenade, peaceful at dusk – before the nighttime revels begin.

Below: A traditional merry-go-round on Brighton beach offers old-fashioned seaside entertainment. More modern amusements are to be found on the end of the pier, including a funfair with a Superbooster ride that propels participants from zero to 60mph in less than 3 seconds.

Opposite page: The land to the south of Chichester is so flat, and intervening developments so low in profile, that the Gothic spire of the city's medieval cathedral can be used as a landmark for sailors out in the Channel. Unusually, the cathedral's bells have always been housed in a completely separate, specially built bell tower – a feature that is unique in England.

Right: The postmill above the village of Clayton on the South Downs is named Jill – her partner, a brick-built tower mill is, of course, Jack. Female names for windmills are apparently the norm, and Jill still grinds corn for the benefit of visitors.

Right: A boardwalk leads through the powdery white sand at West Wittering, a Blue Flag-quality beach by Chichester Harbour.

Below, left and right: Arundel Castle is the historic seat of the Earls of Arundel. Originating in medieval times, it resigned gracefully into the status of a domestic stately home some time after the 12th century, and extensive restoration in the 18th and 19th centuries ensured a reasonably high level of comfort for its inhabitants.

Opposite page: Arundel's Roman Catholic cathedral was built in a French Gothic style, and founded by the prominent Howard family in the 19th century. The building is dedicated to Our Lady and St Philip Howard, the 20th Earl of Arundel who was martyred for his faith in the 16th century and canonized in 1970.

Overleaf: The view north from the South Downs Way National Trail overlooks the village of Fulking, inland from Hove. The long distance footpath stretches 100 miles (161km) from Winchester in the west to Eastbourne, on the Sussex coast.

Left: Newcastle has a splendid clutch of bridges over the River Tyne. The tilting footbridge known locally as 'the blinking eye' is the latest, opened in 2000 to link to the silvery Sage concert hall in Gateshead. Behind this can be seen the Tyne suspension bridge (1928), the low swing bridge (1876) and Robert Stephenson's double-decker High Level Bridge (1849), which carries a railway on the upper deck and a road on the lower.

Below: Antony Gormley's iconic steel statue, the *Angel of the North*, dominates the hill above Gateshead with a wingspan to match a jumbo jet. Since its completion in 1998 it has briefly been clad in a Newcastle United football team shirt, but otherwise stands exposed to the elements, its feet firmly planted in some 600 tonnes of concrete.

Opposite page: Oliver Cromwell's Parliamentarians used the Church of St Nicholas at Alcester as barracks during the Civil War, even stabling their horses in the building until smoked out by rival Royalists in 1644. By the 18th century it needed substantial repair, and was largely rebuilt. The clock is unusually positioned on a corner of the tower, where it can be easily seen from the town's high street.

Left: The extraordinary windmill at Chesterton, near Warwick, dates to around 1632 and stands on six stone piers, gazing out over the Warwickshire countryside. Despite its water-tower appearance and domed observatory-style roof, it really was planned as a mill to grind corn, by local landowner Edward Peyto.

Below: Picturesque Warwick Castle looks satisfyingly just as a medieval castle should, set on a dreamy curve of the River Avon. It was King Alfred's daughter, Ethelfleda, who first spotted the potential of the site in AD914, but the structure seen today relects significant rebuilding in the 17th century. Queens Elizabeth I and Victoria both visited the castle. Edward IV was a less willing visitor, imprisoned here in 1469.

Right: A lovestruck Robert Dudley, favourite of Elizabeth I, built the red sandstone palace of Kenilworth Castle to impress Her Majesty with his ardour in 1575. There had been a castle here for several centuries before, and its transformation to the atmospheric ruin we see today came in the 17th century, when a Parliamentarian force blew it up to avoid further trouble. Its romantic status was reinforced by novelist Walter Scott, who retold the tale of the Queen's visit in his eponymous novel of 1826, putting Kenilworth firmly on the tourist map.

Below: In 1582 William Shakespeare married Anne Hathaway. This is her family home in Shottery near Stratford-upon-Avon, now known as Anne Hathaway's Cottage, but then just plain Newlands Farm. An exact replica of this Tudor delight was constructed by enthusiasts on Vancouver Island, Canada, in 1959.

Left: Open-air museums don't come much better than the Black Country Living Museum in Dudley, which preserves around 60 industrial buildings of significance from all over the West Midlands. They are peopled by a cast of actors and skilled craftspeople, recreating a glimpse of an age when the Industrial Revolution fully exploited the natural resources of this area. Highlights include the 1930s canal dock, the anchor forge and the old locksmith's house.

Below: Birmingham's Gas Street Basin was the motorway service station of its day – for canal barges carrying their cargoes through the congested arteries of the city, and swapping their loads manually from one waterway to another. There are still canalside pubs here for the pleasure craft which moor up.

Opposite page: Like something dreamed up on the set of TV's *Dr Who*, the bobbled alien form of the Selfridges building forms a vast silver bulge on Birmingham's Bull Ring shopping centre. Its construction in 2003 included a coating of 15,000 aluminium discs, and reflects a modern architectural style that has been nicknamed 'blobitecture'.

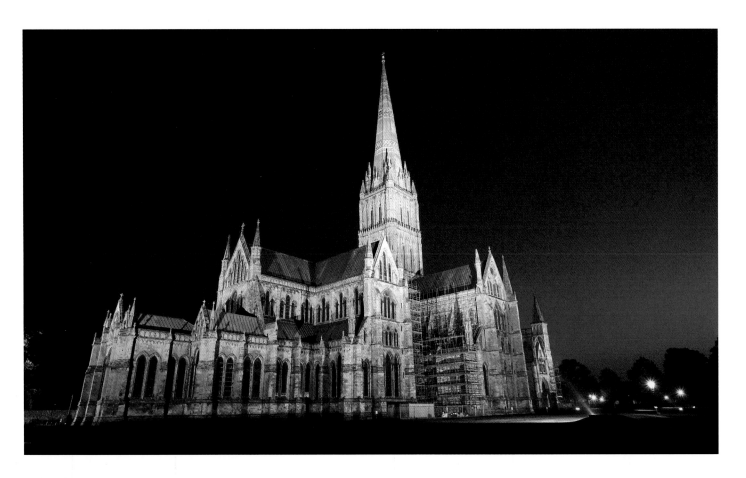

Opposite page, above: Salisbury Cathedral was built with remarkable rapidity, in less than 40 years after 1220. The graceful spire, the highest in England at 404ft (123m), was added in 1320, and featured in several well-known paintings by 19th-century landscape artist John Constable.

Opposite page, below: Castle Combe in Wiltshire is often claimed to be the prettiest village in England, with its market cross, its Cotswold stone cottages and its bubbling stream completing the picture, which is familiar from a dozen calendars.

Left: Engineer John Rennie's solution, when his Kennet and Avon Canal was blocked by the River Avon, was to build an elegant aqueduct. Avoncliff was constructed in 1797, and the main stone arch has shown an unfortunate tendency, over time, to sag in the middle. In recent repairs, the leaky clay lining was replaced with concrete. Rennie's second aqueduct, at Dundas, has stood the test of time slightly better.

Below: Long Kennet's barrow was built around 3650BC, eventually holding some 50 bodies. The stones, now exposed, would once have been covered by a long earthwork. Archaeologists hoped that nearby Silbury Hill, to the right of this photo, might reveal more burials, but excavations have found nothing, and its purpose remains a mystery.

Overleaf: The Westbury White Horse stands patiently on the escarpment overlooking Salisbury Plain. One of a dozen to be found etched into the chalky Wiltshire hills, its modern appearance is thanks to George Gee, who had it remodelled and recut in 1778. A coating of concrete and white paint in the 1990s has ensured its maintenance as a distinctive local landmark.

Opposite page: 'Capability' Brown was the great landscape gardener of the 18th century, remodelling landscapes across England to emphasise the picturesque. His viewing tower on the Cotswold escarpment near Broadway makes the most of its location 1,024ft (312m) above sea level. Enemy aircraft were tracked from its high battlements during the Second World War.

Below, left: Pershore Abbey is an oddly truncated structure huddled up to its sturdy tower. When part of it collapsed in the 17th century, a blocking wall was simply built to fill the gap, and the tumbled masonry carted away. The peal of eight bells in the tower is famous for its mellow tone. Church bells are a tribute to the founders' art and are often marked with the name of their donor. One here is inscribed: 'I to the church the living call and to the grave do summon all 1729'.

Below, right: The 8-mile (13km) ridge of the Malvern Hills sticks up out of the plains of Worcestershire and Herefordshire, and were once famed for their natural mineral springs. They form a spectacular playground for walkers and horse riders, and attract adrenaline sports such as hang-gliding.

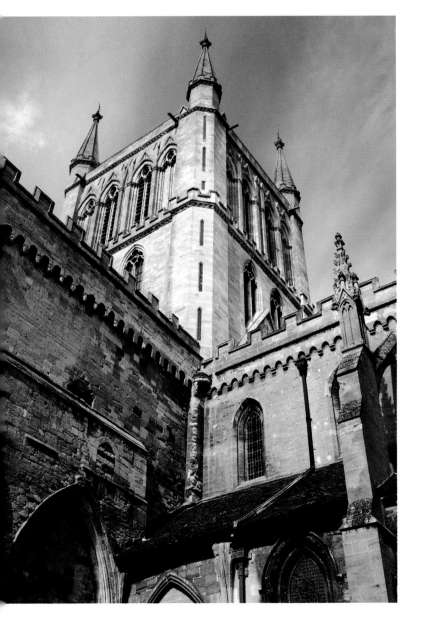

Right: The rugged chalk cliffs at Bempton, on the East Yorkshire coast, provide natural tower-block dwellings for a myriad of breeding seabirds in early summer. Puffins, razorbills, guillemots and gannets are among the noisy tenants who make the most of the crevices and narrow ledges eroded into the rock. The RSPB maintains a reserve on the cliff top.

Below: Dodgem cars provide the fun of the fair at Bridlington, a Victorian holiday resort on the east coast. The town's landmark Spa Pavilion, which became known for its ballroom and resident dance band in the 1930s, reopened in 2008 as a venue for popular rock concerts.

Bottom: The chalky point of Flamborough Head gained its first lighthouse in 1674. The current, automated light was built close by in 1806, and designed by Samuel Wyatt. A further extension in 1925 added to its height.

Right: Skipton Castle is one of the most complete and best-preserved medieval castles in England. It stands at the top of this historic market town's high street, and was the birthplace of the indomitable Lady Anne Clifford, whose diary of her life and travels across the country sheds a particular light on aristocratic life in the 17th century.

Below: Semer Water is Yorkshire's largest natural lake. It was formed in Rydale during the ice age, when a retreating glacier left behind a huge clay dam, and another was blocked in by a glacier in Wensleydale. The resultant meltwater formed Semer Water, now ringed by the three villages of Countersett, Marsett and Stalling Busk.

Left: Grikes (crevices) wrinkle the windswept surface of the exposed limestone 'pavement' at the top of Malham Cove, giving a grip to unusual alpine plants. The Cove itself, a notable magnet for climbers, is a cliff, 250ft (76m), curving into a natural amphitheatre.

Below: Typical red-tiled cottages in the fishing hamlet of Cowbar, on the North Yorkshire coast. Little houses stretch out along the headland of Cow Nab, separated from the larger village of Staithes by a small river, or beck. Moored in front is a traditional wooden fishing boat known as a Whitby cobble, used to catch lobsters and crabs as well as sea fish.

Below: Narrow York stone pillars separated by stained glass support the magnificent vaulted wooden roof of the octagonal Chapter House of York Minster. It dates to around 1260, and is completed with a gilded central boss depicting the Lamb of Christ.

Opposite page: The soaring twin towers of York Minster, England's finest Gothic cathedral, frame the magnificent tracery of the West Window. Some of the best medieval glass in the world is to be seen here, including the vast and colourful East Window of 1408, and the narrow, sober grey lancets of the Five Sisters.

Right: Straw bales catch the evening light in a field in Nidderdale, near the village of Pately Bridge, with the high moors behind. The Nidderdale Way, a 53-mile (85km) circular trail, winds around the valley.

Below: The extensive monastic remains of Rievaulx Abbey, on the edge of the North Yorkshire Moors near Helmsley, give an indication of the scale and wealth of the Cistercian community that established itself here in the 12th century. Up to 140 monks and 600 lay brothers farmed sheep, cultivated vegetables and crops, and smelted iron here, on the banks of the River Rye, until the Dissolution in the 16th century brought it all to an end.

Below, left and right: Old and new in the city of Sheffield. To the left are the elegant Grecian-style pillars of the City Hall, which was built in the 1930s. In front is the bronze base of the city's First World War memorial, set on the square known as Barker's Pool. High-rise tower blocks in the right-hand picture reflect the switch in this once-mighty industrial city, built on steelworks, to redevelopment as a centre for service industries in the 21st century.

Left: In front of Sheffield's Victorian Town Hall spread the Peace Gardens, a modern square full of fountains and cascades. This miniature park occupies the site of an old churchyard, and is a sign of the city's rejuvenation at the end of the 20th century. The Goodwin Fountain, named after a local steel magnate, is the central focus.

Below: Victoria Hall Methodist Church is located in the city centre, and recalls the heyday of the Methodist movement in Yorkshire. It is a generously proportioned building, with a solid-looking red-brick tower and dressed stone frontage. It was built in 1906 and has been at the heart of welfare projects in Sheffield from the start, when poverty was rife and jobs few. This spirit continues today, with free meals provided at the church for homeless people.

Right, below and opposite page: Titus Salt was a paternal Leeds-born wool merchant who decided that the best way was his way. Accordingly, he constructed a 'model' village for his textile factory workers, removing them from slum dwellings and combining care for their welfare with a shrewd business sense of people management. With its buildings of pale gold stone reflecting the Italianate style so popular here in the mid-19th century, Saltaire has a charm and completeness about it, and is now preserved as a World Heritage Site. As you explore, you can see neatly laid out terraced houses built for his workers, and the larger houses for middle and senior management. Streets are named after Salt's wife Caroline and 11 children. The vast mill building on the bank of the River Aire (left) is now a smart art gallery with a dedicated collection by Bradford-born artist David Hockney. The cottage hospital and church (this page) can be easily identified. There was also a school, and a park for recreation.

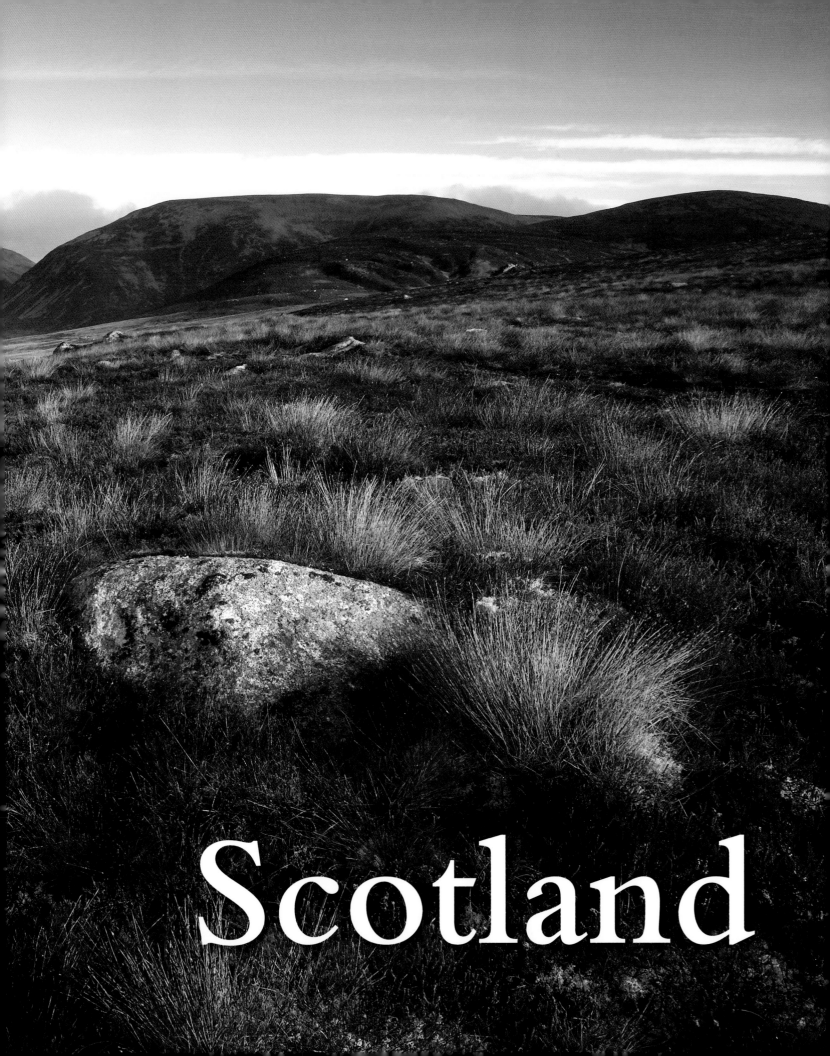

Scotland

Previous pages: The wild uplands of the Cairngorm Mountains are protected as part of Scotland's second National Park. This view was taken in Gleann an t-Slugain, looking towards Beinn a'Bhuird peak on the far left of the image.

Left and below: David I founded Melrose Abbey in 1136, and Robert the Bruce's heart is buried beneath its floor. The Douglas family later robbed it of some of its stones to build a house nearby, and the ruin might have continued unchecked had not Sir Walter Scott stepped in, instigating repairs in the 19th century. Vivid carvings (see below) on the romantic red sandstone ruin include saints, dragons, flowers, and a pig playing the bagpipes.

Below: From the hills above Tweedsmuir, the Talla Water flows down into the valley and is trapped in a reservoir, serving Edinburgh. The Talla Waterworks Scheme, which started in the last year of the 19th century, required many labourers, some of whom came from Ireland to help build the necessary railway link. Around 30 of them died during the construction, and remain buried in Tweedsmuir kirkyard.

Right: Where the waters of Loch Skeen tumble over the alpine heights above the Moffat glen, a spectacular 200ft (60m) waterfall, the Grey Mare's Tail, is formed.

Below: A high harbour wall shelters the fishing village of St Abbs, in southeast Scotland, from the worst of the North Sea storms. Clear waters make this a popular diving spot, and Britain's first Voluntary Marine Reserve was created just offshore in the 1980s to preserve the richly diverse local marine life.

Opposite page: Lonely Hermitage Castle looms above a marsh, south of the Borders town of Hawick. Its grim lack of windows makes it clear that this was a fortress designed for fighting and foul deeds. One owner was boiled alive for crimes of witchcraft and murder, while another starved his rival to death in the castle dungeon, before meeting his own grisly death in the nearby woods.

Overleaf: A geographical fault line in the hills behind St Abbs left a marshy depression, now flooded to form the Mire Loch. It has become a valuable freshwater addition to the local nature reserve, a base for little grebes and swans, as well as reed buntings.

Right and below: The Lake of Menteith is a beauty spot near Aberfoyle, its sparkling waters filling a saucer-shaped depression left by a retreating glacier in the ice age. It is so shallow that it has been known to freeze over in recent years, allowing the game of curling to take place on the ice. Port of Menteith, at the eastern end, is the main settlement, with a hotel for fishing folk and a little ferry boat that brings curious visitors to the lake's biggest island: Inchmahome. Step ashore here to discover the considerable remains of a 13th-century Augustinian priory hidden among the trees. Kings Robert the Bruce and Robert II visited, and in 1547, at the age of just four, a fugitive Mary, Queen of Scots was concealed here for several weeks. The monks became a victim of the Scottish Reformation, and the monastery gradually crumbled until passed to the care of Historic Scotland in 1926.

Below: Autumnal birches catch the light in Achray Forest, which lies to the north of Aberfoyle in the Trossachs. The distant peak of Ben Ledi is the highest point around, at 2,884ft (879m). Achray includes an area of wetland, the Blackwater Marshes, where wildfowl such as goosander, wigeon and teal may be seen, and is managed by the Forestry Commission as part of the Queen Elizabeth Forest Park.

Right: Two small steamships regularly ply the tranquil waters of Loch Katrine, at the heart of the Trossachs. They are named after Sir Walter Scott and his epic poem, *The Lady of the Lake*, which first drew fans of his work here by the carriage-load in the 19th century.

Left: Ben Venue is mirrored in the still waters of Loch Achray, which lies to the west of Callander. Views from the mountain top reach as far as the islands of Arran and Jura on a clear day. The little Trossachs Church, dating to 1849, lies on the shore of the loch, and its scenic location makes it a favourite for weddings.

Below: Red deer roam the moors and mountains of Scotland, and their roaring can echo through the glens during the autumn rutting season. Britain's largest land mammal, they have no natural predators left in the wild, but are hunted by man for their venison and to control their numbers. The tawny fur which gives them their name fades to a greyer shade in winter.

Bottom: The Hielan' coo (Highland cow) with its shaggy coat and bemused expression is a comical emblem of Scotland. In fact, these sturdy animals are the ideal all-weather, all-terrain beef cow, and their wide horns belie a gentle temperament that has seen them exported successfully to countries all around the world, including Finland, Argentina and Switzerland.

Left, opposite: The remnants of three round towers mark out the triangular castle of Caerlaverock, on the Solway Firth to the southeast of Dumfries. This handsome 13th-century fortress was the home of the Maxwell family, who built stately rooms within its protective walls.

Left, above and below: Cicstercian monks founded Glenluce Abbey in the peaceful Luce Valley in 1192. Its Chapter House remains intact, but the rest has fallen into genteel ruin. This carved face of a Green Man, with leaves sprouting from his mouth, may be seen in the roof structure of the Chapter House; such mythological figures are taken to represent rebirth in the cycle of life.

Below: Trees line the edge of Loch Ken, an 11-mile (18km) stretch of fresh water between New Galloway and Newton Stewart, in southwestern Scotland. The RSPB manages a marsh here, and reintroduced red kites into the area in 2003. You can watch these distinctive birds of prey in the wild, or see them fly into the feeding station at Bellymack Hill Farm, near Laurieston.

Right: An obelisk tops Whita Hill, above the village of Langholm. It is the Malcolm Memorial, dedicated to soldier and statesman John Malcolm, who was born on a nearby farm in 1769. Malcolm made his name in India, in a distinguished career serving with the army and as a diplomat.

Below: The roofless remains of St Ninian's Chapel occupy an isolated corner of the far southwest of Scotland, the Isle of Whithorn. This simple rectangular building was erected in the 13th century, on the medieval pilgrimage trail to Whithorn Abbey, where the faithful came in search of a miracle cure for leprosy.

Opposite page: Maclellan's Castle is a fortified L-plan tower house at the centre of the charming artists' town of Kirkcudbright. It was built at the end of the 16th century by Thomas Maclellan of Bombie, and passed eventually to the Maxwells, who removed the roof and stripped out the lintels and metalwork in the 18th century, and left the stonework to fend for itself. It is remarkably intact, considering its history, and a testament to careful construction.

Below, left and right: Before the Reformation, St Andrews was the ecclesiastical and scholarly capital of Scotland, and it boasts the country's oldest university, founded in 1413. St Salvatore's College (below right, and detail, left) became part of this in 1450, and some of its fine medieval buildings are still in daily use. It is built around a quadrangle, and is the focus for the traditionally riotous Raisin Monday festivities, when first year students give thanks to older students in the tangible form of bottles of wine.

Overleaf: Lobster pots line the harbour at Pittenweem, the chief fisheries port for the East Neuk of Fife. St Filian based himself here in the 7th century, while converting the local Picts to Christianity. Its delightful miniature cottages and narrow lanes provide endless prospects for artists.

Opposite page, above: A century after John Knox preached at St Andrews Cathedral in 1669, the Reformation had swept through Scotland and the buildings were left derelict. The crumbled remains are dramatically set beside the sea, and you can climb the tower of St Rule's Church for eye-popping views.

Opposite page, below: The firm sweep of the West Sands at St Andrews leads straight onto the famous golf course. The town is the home of the Royal and Ancient Golf Club, founded in 1754 and still the ruling authority on the game worldwide. The Open Championship, one of the four most prestigious international golfing tournaments, is played out here every five years or so.

Left: An alleyway in the beautifully preserved town of Culross. Poverty preserved this gem on the Forth, as it was bypassed by the industrial growth of the 19th century and remained a backwater. In the 1930s the National Trust for Scotland started buying up the near-derelict properties, and decades later many of the houses are fully restored and lived in by ordinary folk.

Below: The squat Auld Kirk (old church) stands alone at the western end of St Monans, a tiny Fife fishing village otherwise crowded around its harbour. The church was built by David II in the 14th century, and remains so close to the sea that it is a wonder it has not been washed away. St Monance, for whom it is named, was a local saint killed by marauding Vikings around AD875.

Opposite page: Crail is the easternmost of the string of pretty fishing villages preserved along the southern coastline of Fife. Former trading links with the Low Countries are revealed in the architectural details here: orange pantile roofs and high, crow-stepped gables. The square-towered Tolbooth even has a Dutch bell, cast in 1520.

Opposite page: A lantern powered by whale oil and perched on one corner of the high walls of Kinnaird Castle, Fraserburgh, became Scotland's first lighthouse in 1787. It is now the centrepiece of the Museum of Scottish Lighthouses, and gives grand views over the fishing harbour.

Below: Immaculate topiary and formal bedding characterize the garden at Pitmedden, near Ellon, started by Alexander Seton in 1675. The garden is extensive, boasting more than 5 miles (8km) of box hedging – quite a feat of manicuring for the team of National Trust for Scotland gardeners. Stone sundials and fountains give focus to the parterres of this recreated Renaissance wonder.

Right: The Town House on Aberdeen's Castle Street is typical of the bold 19th-century granite structures of Scotland's third city. Aberdeen started life as a trading port and seaside resort, but is better known today as the oil capital of Europe.

Opposite page: Thomas Telford's cast iron bridge at Craigellachie, near Aberlour, has been carrying traffic across the Spey safely since 1814. Indeed, the superior height of this delicate-looking construction meant it was the only bridge across the river to survive the massive floods of 1829, when lesser structures were washed away. It's still used by walkers and cyclists, but heavier vehicles and road rerouting called for a solid concrete neighbour in the 1970s.

Left: A bronze figure representing *Victory and Peace* tops the magnificent war memorial in the High Street of Elgin. In her left hand she clutches a laurel wreath symbolizing living memory. Bronze plaques wrapped around the base record the names of the dead of the First World War, the majority of whom served with the Seaforth Highlanders.

Below: The town of Elgin presents a smart, bustling 19th-century face to the world, but its origins are much older, as revealed by the ruins of its medieval cathedral. This huge structure was abandoned in the 16th century, and stripping the valuable lead from its roof in 1567 led to rapid decay (the lead was to be sold in Holland to raise money for a private army, but got no further than Aberdeen Harbour, where it sank with its ship). Yet the high walls remain remarkably intact, giving an impression of strength against adversity.

Below: Pennan's single row of cottages backed up against the cliff, with a small hotel in the middle, will be instantly familiar to fans of the 1983 movie *Local Hero*, which was filmed here. It's located on the northern coastline of Aberdeenshire, along with several other isolated fishing communities with their access strictly limited by the steep cliffs. Millstones were quarried from the stone here in the 19th century.

Opposite page: A profusion of flowering herbaceous borders surround the fairytale towers of Crathes Castle. It was built at the end of the 16th century near Banchory, on the boggy site of a much older castle, and remained in the Burnett family until passed into the care of National Trust for Scotland in the 1950s. One of Crathes' treasures is the ancient bejewelled Horn of Leys, which adds to the mystical air – it was a gift, along with the land to build the castle, of Robert the Bruce in 1323.

Overleaf: A narrow, windswept promontory is all that links Dunnottar Castle to the mainland. Blasted by North Sea winds, its ruins evoke a harsh past. The Scottish regalia – the crown, orb and sceptre, now held in Edinburgh Castle – were held here for safety during the Civil War, and the men of Dunnottar withstood an eight-month siege to protect them from a Parliamentary force. They ultimately lost the battle, but the crown jewels were smuggled out to safety. Dunnottar was the home of the powerful Earls Marischal, until the last one backed the losing side in the Jacobite Rebellion of 1715 and it was abandoned to the elements.

Right: The golden eagle is Britain's largest bird of prey, and rarely seen outside Scotland. They prefer to live in wide open spaces, well away from human populations, so walkers in remote corners have perhaps the best chance of spotting them. With a wingspan of almost 6ft (2m), they are unmistakable.

Below: At 4,406ft (1,343m) Ben Nevis is the highest mountain in Britain, but often hides its tops in cloud. Some of the best views of the shy peak can be had from Corpach, where the Caledonian Canal disgorges into Loch Linnhe. The canal was engineered by Thomas Telford in the early 19th century to link the waterways of the Great Glen and give safer access to the eastern seaboard at Inverness.

Above: Granite boulders, weathered and tossed during the upheavals of the last ice age provide a challenge for walkers and climbers in the eastern Cairngorms. This one can be found in a corrie near the plateau of Ben Avon, which looms 3,842ft (1,171m) to the north of Braemar.

Left: The red squirrel is Britain's native species, constantly under threat from expanding populations of their rival grey cousins. You are more likely to see them in Scotland than elsewhere in Britain – in the woodlands of Perthshire and Speyside, for example, and forest parks across the country, where they thrive on tree seeds and nuts.

Overleaf: Dawn light catches the bleak beauty of the peaks to the west of Ben Macdhui, in the heart of the Cairngorm Mountains. This remote area became part of Scotland's second National Park, created in 2003.

Left: Urquhart Castle, strategically set on the northern shore of tranquil Loch Ness, suffered a turbulent history. It was fought over many times – not just in battles between the Scots and the English, but also in the fierce power struggles between the great Scottish families, or clans. Today it is a picturesque ruin that provides a great base for modern day monster-hunters.

Below: Oxeye daisies grow wild in the hedgerows and along the roadsides of the Highlands and the rest of Britain, bringing a splash of summer colour from May onwards. Much bigger and bolder than the common daisy, they are also known as dogdaisies.

Right: At the head of Glenfinnan stands a monument to commemorate the landing of Prince Charles Edward Stuart here in 1745. Better known in legend as Bonnie Prince Charlie, he had come from exile to raise an army and restore his father to the throne of Scotland. The generic kilted Highlander on top of the pillar gazes out over Loch Shiel.

Below: Suilven peak peeps out to the right of Cul Mor in Inverpolly National Nature Reserve. Both mountains in this remote part of northwest Scotland were purchased by the local community in 2005, as part of the Glencanisp and Drumrunie estates, and are now managed by the Assynt Foundation.

Opposite page: The steep valley of Glencoe, in the western Highlands, is haunted by the memory of a massacre which took place here in 1692, between the Campbells and the MacDonalds, and all in the King's name. Roadside pipers, busking for the tourist buses, help to build up the eerie atmosphere. These mountains are a popular challenge for climbers, and claim additional lives every year.

Right: The Cuillin Hills form the backbone of Skye, with Blaven standing 3,041ft (927m) high. The Red Cuillins are of pink, scree-covered granite, while the jagged Black Cuillins consist of gabbro, an igneous rock similar to basalt. The island boasts twelve Munros – that is, peaks designated to be over 3,000ft (914m) – making them a mountaineer's paradise.

Below: Travelling 'over the sea to Skye' became a whole lot simpler in 1995 when the controversial bridge at Kyle of Lochalsh opened, rendering at least one ferry route obsolete. You can still catch the boat from Mallaig, or in summer to Kylerhea.

Right: Founded as a physic garden for medicinal purposes in the 17th century, Edinburgh's Royal Botanic garden covers 70 acres (28ha) of landscaped and wooded ground to the north of the city, and includes the largest collection of Chinese plants to be found outside China. These dish-like, giant Victoria waterlilies flourish in the tropical warmth of the vast glasshouse.

Below: Ornamental iron gates protect the Palace of Holyroodhouse, the Queen's official residence in Edinburgh.

Opposite page, top left: This distinctive gilded sign hangs outside Gladstone's Land, a restored 17th-century tenement in Edinburgh's Old Town. Thomas Gledstanes bought the place in 1617; 'gled' is the Scots word for a hawk. Today the site has been preserved and restored by the National Trust for Scotland.

Opposite page, top right: An elegant Georgian entrance marks out a terraced house in Queen Street. This broad street runs parallel with Princes Street and is a highlight of Edinburgh's gracious New Town, which was built in the mid-18th century.

Opposite page, below: Built into the cobblestones of the Royal Mile, just outside St Giles' Cathedral, is this curious symbol. It is the Heart of Midlothian, and owes its existence to the romantic writer Sir Walter Scott, who wrote a stirring novel of the same name in 1818. It marks the location of the Old Tolbooth, at one time a notorious prison and place of public execution.

Left: A view over the Scottish capital by night, from the top of Calton Hill. Waverley Bridge and the 'crown' of St Giles' Cathedral can be seen to the left, with the castle ahead, and the spire of the Scott Memorial clearly visible on Princes Street, overshadowed by the floodlit tower of the Balmoral Hotel. In the foreground is the memorial by William Playfair to Dugald Stewart, a noted mathematician and philosopher born in the city, who died in 1828.

Right: The bare green hill of Arthur's Seat forms the bottom of Edinburgh's Old Town ridge, looming 823ft (251m) high and visible for miles around. It's the remains of a volcano 325 million years old, with seven smaller hills around it, and the high cliffs of Salisbury Crag, tilted in a later ice age.

Below: Edinburgh's most famous landmark, the castle, attracts around a million visitors a year, and the Military Tattoo which takes over the Esplanade each summer, complete with skirling pipe bands, is televised around the world. The site, perched impregnably on a volcanic plug of rock, has been occupied since the Bronze Age, and the first castle was built in the Middle Ages. The views from the walls over the city and beyond are breathtaking.

Overleaf: The Forth Rail Bridge is an impressive structure from any angle, and became an icon soon after its construction, which began in 1890 and took eight years. Maintaining its red oxide paintwork was a notoriously never-ending task, but a recent coating of modern materials, including layers of glass flake epoxy and polyurethane, promise to give a more durable and lasting finish.

Opposite page: The Ring of Brodgar is a wide circle of 27 standing stones, surrounded by a ditch, and lying on a narrow strip of land between the lochs of Harray and Stenness, on the Mainland. It was built in Neolithic times, around 2500BC, and is just one of several significant ancient sites in the immediate area.

Left: The Scottish thistle is found growing across the country, and was adopted as an emblem of Scottish pride back in the 13th century. Legend has it that an army of soft-footed Norse invaders revealed their presence when they trod on the prickly plants in the dark, waking the Scottish defenders and so preventing a rout. James V created the first chivalric Order of the Thistle in 1540, and it remains the gift of the monarch today.

Below: The island of Hoy, seen here across the bay from Orkney's Mainland, derives its name from the Old Norse term *Ha-ey*, meaning 'high island'. Its tall cliffs offer attractive breeding grounds for puffins, great skuas and raptors such as hen harriers.

Right: Stromness harbour lies bathed in summer sunlight. Orkney, like Shetland, shares a close history with Scandinavia and tends to regard itself as a part of Britain which is separate from Scotland. The islands became part of Scotland in the 15th century, granted as a dowry when Margaret of Denmark married James III. Although the islands ring with Norse-sounding place names, Picts and Celts predated the Vikings here by at least 3,500 years.

Below: Dazzling stonework on St Magnus Cathedral, in the Orkney 'capital' of Kirkwall. This vast red sandstone structure was started by Earl Ragnvald in 1137 and dedicated to his murdered great-uncle, St Magnus. It is the focus for an annual music festival, started in 1977 by composer Peter Maxwell Davies, who has adopted Orkney as his home.

Below right: In 1850, a great storm swept away sands on the shore at Sandwick on Orkney's Mainland, revealing the remains of a stone-built village, Scara Brae. Buried since another such storm in Neolithic times, chambered houses were linked with winding walkways, the walls shored up by midden which gave both shelter and insulation. Excavations allow you to look down into the homes, complete with stone slab furnishings.

Opposite page: The Old Man of Hoy is a sandstone stack off the western cliffs of Hoy. Standing 450ft (37m) tall, it is a popular challenge for climbers. Mountaineer Chris Bonington was the first to climb to the top, as one of a team of three in 1966. Isolated on its basalt perch, this famous landmark is vulnerable to erosion by sea and wind, and will one day topple.

Previous pages: Moo Stack, by the cliffs at Eshaness, has been created by the pounding Atlantic waves that crash around Shetland Mainland's western extremity. It's a wild coastline, carved into deep clefts and voes, the result of a volcano that erupted around 350 million years ago.

Right and below: At Jarlshof, near the southern tip of Shetland, an ancient broch was adapted some time during the Iron Age to form the hub of a wheel-shaped communal roundhouse. The Vikings, also into communal living, built a vast longhouse close by in the 9th century. Grander lairds built individual houses here in later centuries. Archaeologists are still peeling away the layers of human history at this fascinating site. Sheep farming has been part of the scene for thousands of years, with Viking remains showing that weavers had their looms here. Today drystone fanks, or pens, are used for gathering and sorting the sheep (below), but overlay what may be signs of earlier strip farming.

Opposite page: Brochs – double-skinned circular towers – are a Scottish phenomenon, and that at Mousa island, off southern Shetland, is the most complete example you could wish to see. It dates to around 100BC, and probably played a defensive role at some time, but nobody can be sure. Now storm petrels nest in the neat stonework.

Right: Lerwick may be the modern 'capital' of Shetland, but in medieval times this role fell to Scalloway, to the west. The castle of 1599, now a ruin, occupies a superb defensive position with the sea on three sides. At one time it would have been surrounded by outbuildings and walls, but little remains except the gaunt tower house, overlooking the modern harbour.

Below: A tough climate requires hardy domestic breeds, and Shetland has several strains of wiry sheep, perfectly suited to its environment. Nothing can be cuter, however, than the Shetland pony, its diminutive size giving it kiddie appeal worldwide. These gruff, compact little workhorses were bred in the 19th century and into the 20th for work down the coal mines, but are now more likely to be seen bouncing novice riders along rather than hauling loads.

Left: Grey seals are a familiar sight in the waters around Shetland, their Roman noses distinguishing them from their fellow common seals. The old Shetland name was 'haaf fish', or 'deep fish', for their habit of diving in deep, open waters, but this one, snapped in Lerwick Harbour, was probably after the scraps from the local fish processing factories.

Below: Remote Foula is the most westerly of the Shetland islands, separated from the main group by a reef, the Shaalds of Foula, which has caught out many an unwary navigator over the centuries. Although a handful of people live here and farm their crofts year-round, seabirds are the main inhabitants.

Right: This intriguing pock–marked boulder at Nether Largie is one of dozens of ancient remains that litter the peaceful Kilmartin Glen, in Argyll. Nobody knows who sculpted the shallow circular hollows on this menhir – or exactly why, although it's a form of prehistoric decoration seen widely.

Left: Loch Awe is a 23-mile (37km) finger of fresh water among the forested Argyll hills. The clear waters teem with trout and pike. At its marshy northern end sits the picturesque ruin of Kilchurn Castle, built by Colin Campbell of Breadalbane in the 1440s.

Below: The beautiful coastline of Appin is scattered with islands and inlets, a bloody battleground in centuries gone by when clans fought each other for control of the seaways. Castle Stalker, a four-storey tower house on its own rocky islet, dating to the mid-15th century and silhouetted in the centre of this page, is a scenic reminder of these turbulent times.

Right: A view to the Black Mount across an ice-bound Rannoch Moor, in the Western Highlands. The moor is a boggy expanse that can feel like the end of the Earth on a bleak day. Its superb isolation makes Rannoch a vital habitat for rare species of plants and insects.

Below: Philanthropic banker John Stuart McCaig wanted to create a family memorial and relieve local unemployment at the end of the 19th century, in his home-town of Oban. He commissioned the great drum-shaped granite tower that now bears his name, to be built on a hilltop overlooking the bay. Perhaps fortunately, he died before the museum could be built inside, or statues placed in every niche, for today McCaig's Folly offers perfect little frames for the view over the harbour to the hills and islands beyond.

This page: The architecture and designs of Charles Rennie Mackintosh have been adopted and celebrated as Glasgow style in recent years. Mackintosh was born in the city in 1865, and his most magnificent legacy is surely the School of Art on Renfrew Street (below, left and right). With its confident modern lines and bold, unusual decorative details, it is still very much in use, influencing generations of art students. In 1904 Mackintosh was commissioned by Kate Cranston to design the interiors of several tea shops in Glasgow, of which the Willow Tearooms, in Sauchiehall Street, is the most elegant surviving example. Mirrored walls in the upstairs Salon de Luxe (above, right) were inset with purple glass and reflected tall-backed silver chairs, providing a genteel backdrop for well-heeled ladies to meet over light refreshments.

Opposite page: Glasgow's premier collection of art and artefacts is displayed in a pink sandstone pile in Kelvingrove Park. With a little of everything, from paintings by Rembrandt and Monet to a stuffed elephant named Sir Roger, there's something in the Kelvingrove Museum for all ages and tastes. Indeed, it claims the most visits per year for any museum outside London. The central hall, in Spanish baroque style and complete with a huge pipe organ, reveals the building's grandiose Victorian origins as a venue for the Glasgow International Exhibition in 1901.

Right: The former Luma light bulb factory, on Shieldhall Road, Glasgow, carried on aspects of the Mackintosh style, although not built until 1938. Its high tower became a well-loved feature of the Govan skyline, and when it looked like it might be demolished in the 1990s, it was fortunately purchased by a housing association and redeveloped as an unusual location for town flats.

Below: The collapse of ship-building in Glasgow in the 20th century meant an opportunity to clean up the River Clyde and to redevelop the docklands at the heart of this great industrial city. The Armadillo – officially the Clyde Auditorium and part of the Scottish Exhibition and Conference Centre – led the way in 1997, on land created by filling in the old Queen's Dock. It is seen reflected here in the glass of the new Science Centre.

Left: The Clyde Arc is the official name given to the 2006 road bridge over the Clyde at Finnieston, close to the Glasgow SECC and Science Centre developments. Less reverential locals know it as the Squinty Bridge, for it is set at a rakish angle across the river. Its central steel bow spans 315ft (96m).

Below: The bulbous form of the IMAX cinema alongside Glasgow's Science Centre is part of the redevelopment of the south bank of the River Clyde, on the former Prince's Dock. Its rounded, titanium- and aluminium-clad form is designed to limit the effects of wind turbulence on the building.

Below: A stone table on the summit of Kinoull Hill, above the town of Perth, affords superb views over the Tay Valley. The Tay is Scotland's longest river, rising in the Western Highlands and flowing into the North Sea beyond Dundee. Perth was built at a point where the river could be crossed at low tide, and named by the Picts for the surrounding woodland – some of which survives on the flanks of Kinoull Hill.

Below: Blair Castle in Perthshire looks just as a Scottish castle should, with white-harled walls, crow-stepped gables and a magnificent setting beneath bare hills, surrounded by mature woodland. It is the home of the Dukes of Atholl, and dominates the main pass between north and south, now followed by both the A9 road and the railway.

Overleaf: It is said by some that Victoria enjoyed the breathtaking panoramic view from this point high above Loch Tummel on one of her many Highland tours. Named Queen's View, it's still a prospect to delight any monarch.

Above: Discovery Point is the focus for the regeneration of Dundee's waterfront, where pride of place is given to the famous heroine of polar exploration, built here in 1900: the Royal Research Ship *Discovery*, which survived being locked in the Antarctic pack ice with Captain Scott. HM Frigate *Unicorn*, in the foreground, was a sailing warship launched in 1824, and is one of the oldest vessels in the world.

Right: This handsome church on the shore above Loch Tay dates to 1760, and forms one end of the central square of the third Earl of Breadalbane's model village at Kenmore. The village today is a popular sailing and watersports centre.

Below: Kisimul Castle is a forbidding medieval fortress in Castlebay, on Barra in the Outer Hebrides. It's the home of the MacNeills, and clan gatherings occur here each year, drawing together members of the wider family who have scattered to all parts of the globe.

Opposite page: The underlying rocks of the Outer Hebrides are some of the oldest in the world. Lewisian gneiss, seen to advantage in the standing stone circle at Callanish, on the Isle of Lewis, is believed to be around 2,900 million years old.

Below: Luminous sands and turquoise sea mark the bay at Uig, in southwest Lewis. In this remote corner in 1831, a set of carved walrus-ivory chess pieces was discovered in the sand. Depicting vivid, pop-eyed Viking figures, they are believed to have been carved in the 12th century and lost soon after, perhaps buried to hide them from Norse raiders.

Opposite page: Dun Carloway, built on a mound above Loch Roag on the Isle of Lewis, reveals a cut-away cross-sectional view of a broch's double skin. Remains at the Iron Age site suggest it was in use as late as the 14th century.

Wales

Previous pages: Glaciers cut the deep mountain valley of Nant Gwynant in the Snowdonia National Park.

Opposite page: Shaggy Kashmiri goats were first released to roam free on the Great Orme peninsula, by Llandudno, in the 19th century, grazing on gorse, brambles and other tough vegetation. The herd is now feral. This sculpture by Graham High guards the visitor centre on the hill top.

Right: Until the Middle Ages trees stood on what is now the bare moorland of Ruabon Mountain near Llangollen. Humans cleared the forest to graze sheep here.

Below: Llandudno is a breezy seaside resort on the north coast of Wales, which was developed during the mid-19th century when the railway boom brought holiday-makers from across the country.

Right: Rhuddlan Castle, on the banks of the River Clwyd in Denbighshire, was built by Edward I and his military architect Master James of St George between 1277 and 1280. Rhuddlan had been the regal base of Welsh ruler Gruffydd ap Llywelyn, but his stronghold was destroyed in 1063 by Harold Godwinson, England's last Anglo-Saxon king.

Below and opposite page: No less than 1,007ft (307m) in length, and running 126ft (38m) above the river, the Pontcysyllte Aqueduct carries the Llangollen Canal between the villages of Froncysyllte and Trevor. Mounted on 19 masonry pillars, it is the longest and highest aqueduct in Britain. It carries the Llangollen Canal across the Dee gorge in a cast-iron trough 11ft (3.4m) wide and 5.25ft (1.60m) deep, with a towpath running alongside.

Opposite page: On the south Pembrokeshire cliffs near Bosherston, the 13th-century St Govan's Chapel marks the place where – according to tradition – a hermit once lived in a crack in the rocks.

Left: Cliffs rise to the south and north, but the central section of St Brides Bay on the Pembrokeshire coast offers an expanse of wide, sandy beaches. The bay, roughly 7 miles (12km) wide, runs between Wooltack Point in the south and St David's Head in the north.

Below: A vast 14-tonne capstone lies atop three 8ft (2.5m) uprights at the Neolithic burial cromlech of Pentre Ifan in the Preseli Hills. Dating to 3500BC the cromlech is unusually aligned north-south, and commands views of the Nevern Valley.

Below: The Pembrokeshire Coast Path runs for 186 miles (299km) between Amroth in the south and St Dogmaels in the north. There are plenty of ups and downs – walking the entire path involves making 35,000ft (10,670m) of climbs and descents. The path delivers breathtaking views and takes in estuaries, coves, windswept clifftops and wide stretches of beach – as here, in St Brides Bay.

Bottom: The Marloes peninsula in the Pembrokeshire Coast National Park– the only coastal national park in Britain.

Right: The marshy, often windswept Preseli Hills in north Pembrokeshire climb to 1,759ft (536m) above sea level at their highest point, Foel Cwmcerwyn. From the rocky tor of Carn Menyn in *c.*2600BC ancient Britons took the great bluestones used in the inner circle of Stonehenge on Salisbury Plain. Historians do not know how the stones, each weighing around 4 tonnes, were transported more than 200 miles (320km).

Right and below: Holidaymakers flock to Tenby, Pembrokeshire's principal resort, which has no fewer than four beaches of pristine golden sand – the North, South, Castle and Harbour beaches. Tenby was a health resort in the Georgian and Victorian eras, and the elegant buildings that look down on the sands are one of the town's enduring attractions.

Opposite page: A 17th-century mill with waterwheel stands beside the Cenarth Falls near Newcastle Emlyn. At this spot salmon attempt to leap up the falls as they try to swim up the River Teifi to spawn, and local tradition has it that 100 salmon were once caught in a single morning's fishing.

Right: The Llyn Nant-y-moch reservoir at Ponterwyd, Ceredigion was created in 1964 as part of the Rheidol hydroelectric power scheme. The nearby moorland of Bryn y Beddau ('Hill of the Graves') contains 200 Welsh dead from the Battle of Nant Hyddgant in 1401, in which Owain Glyndwr's troops defeated Henry IV.

Below: An 11th-century Celtic memorial cross on the roadside near Carew in Pembrokeshire commemorates King Maredudd ap Edwin of the southern Welsh kingdom of Deheubarth, who died in 1035. Carved from local limestone, the cross stands 13ft (4m) tall, and shows Viking influence in the decoration.

Below right: In idyllic Manorbier, south Pembrokeshire, this castle was built in the 12th century by Norman lord Gerald de Barri. He was the father of Manorbier's most famous son, chronicler Gerald of Wales, whose books would become a key source of information for historians of medieval Wales. Gerald was devoted to his birthplace, which he called the 'pleasantest spot in Wales'.

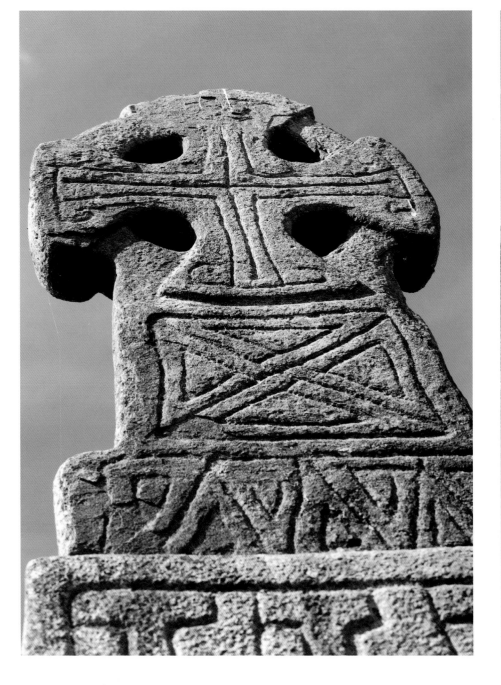

275

Right: Located near Merthyr Tydfil in Mid Glamorgan, the imposing Cefn Coed viaduct was built by engineers Alexander Sutherland and Henry Conybeare in 1866 to carry the railway across the valley of the River Taff. Each arch is 39ft 9in (12.12m) wide and 115ft (35m) tall. It is now used by cyclists following the Taff Trail.

Below: The remains of a sea wall cross the sands at Rest Bay, one of seven beaches at Porthcawl on the coast of south Wales. Initially developed as a port, Porthcawl flourished as a holiday resort from the mid-20th century onwards. Today Rest Bay is a mecca for surfers, with a 'surf cam' enabling enthusiasts to keep an eye on conditions.

Right: Stepping stones over the River Ogmore, beside the remains of Ogmore Castle near Bridgend, Glamorgan, can only be crossed at low tide, and those who venture across should take care, for the stones can be treacherous.

Below: Viewing the atmospheric ruins of Ogmore Castle at sunset, it is easy to believe the legend that King Arthur was fatally wounded here and that his body lies concealed in a nearby cave. The castle builder, William de Londres, was one of the 'Twelve Knights of Glamorgan', a part-historical, part-legendary group of knights who conquered Glamorgan in the service of Norman lord Robert Fitzhamon.

Opposite page: The salt marsh which occurs where the River Ogmore flows into the Atlantic is an eery, unsettling sight in late evening light. The river meets the sea between Ogmore-on-Sea and Merthyr Mawr. To the west miles of sand dunes known as the Merthyr Mawr Warren are known for their rare flora.

Right: The 42-apartment Esplanade House in Porthcawl won an award from the Royal Society of Architects in Wales (RSAW) in 2006, when it was praised for its 'humour, intelligence [and] populism', but locals are far less keen on the colourful building and call it 'the bottle bank'. The design of the block, which stands on the seafront, incorporates marine references including pillars shaped like ice-cream cones.

Opposite page, top: Rows of terraced houses line the sides of the Rhondda Valley, once the centre of the coalmining industry of South Wales. The success of the region's coal mines in the second half of the 19th century spurred a rapid population expansion – from 951 in 1851 to 169,000 in 1924 – and led to the building of the area's characteristic housing.

Opposite page, bottom: The former Lewis Merthyr Colliery in the one-time mining village of Trefahod, south of Porth, is now part of the Rhondda heritage and cultural park. After years of decline, the colliery ended production in 1983. The last operating Rhondda pit, the Maerdy Colliery, closed down in 1990.

Opposite page: The handsome Pierhead Building in Cardiff Bay was built in 1897 by architect William Frame as the headquarters of the Bute Dock Company. The clock tower is known as 'Baby Big Ben' in tribute to the Big Ben clock in Westminster, London. Today the Pierhead is a visitor and conference centre.

Left: As part of a major urban redevelopment of the former docklands, the 150,000sq ft (14,000sq m) Mermaid Quay shopping and leisure centre opened in 1999 on the Cardiff Bay waterfront.

Below: Another imposing new building on the Cardiff Bay waterfront, the Millennium Centre for the performing arts was designed by architect Jonathan Adams. The bilingual inscription on the front includes the English words 'In these stones horizons sing'.

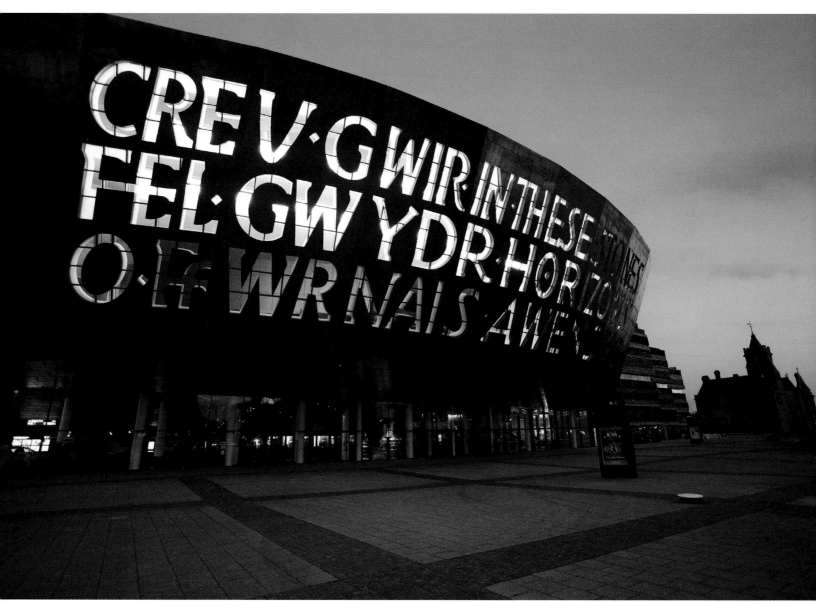

Opposite page and this page, left and below: Lavish interiors were a key part of the Victorian Gothic refurbishment of Cardiff Castle by architect William Burges for John Crichton Stuart, third Marquess of Bute, from 1866 onwards. The castle incorporates the remnants of the original Roman fort and Norman castle on the site. The angel (opposite page) and ceiling carving (below), in the medieval tradition, look down on the Banqueting Hall, while the Arab Room (left) contains a mesmerizing display of patterns inspired by the Islamic decorative tradition.

Below: The last manned lighthouse in Wales, at Nash Point, in the Vale of Glamorgan, was designed by James Walker in 1832 and converted to automatic operation in 1998. It was built on the headland to mark sandbanks at the entrance to the Bristol Channel following the wreck there of the passenger steamer *Frolic* in 1830.

Right: A walk on the beach makes a fascinating excursion at Nash Point, where limestone cliffs rise dramatically above the distinctive wide, sloping rock platforms scoured by the waves, and marine pools lurk invitingly below. The local cliffs are 98-203ft (30-62m) high and often near vertical or even overhanging.

Opposite page: One mile (1.6km) long, Worms Head has a serpentine form as it extends into the waters at the southernmost end of Rhossili Bay on the Gower Peninsula. It takes its name from the Old English Orm meaning 'dragon'. The headland, now a nature reserve, can be reached at low tide along a rocky causeway.

Below: Last light on the beautiful beach of Rhossili Bay catches on the remains of the *Helvetia*, wrecked on the Gower coast in 1887. The Norwegian vessel was bound for Swansea with a load of timber, but after becoming stuck in the bay was washed ashore in a storm. The remains are a distinctive landmark on the beach.

Below: The high, whaleback ridge of Rhossili Downs runs almost the entire length of the beach at Rhossili Bay, protecting the shoreline from development. The Atlantic waves make this a good place for surfers, with the best waves at Llangennith towards the beach's north end.

Opposite page: The cast iron Whiteford Point lighthouse stands off the coast near Whiteford Sands on the Gower Peninsula's northern side, to alert navigators to the shoals of Whiteford Point. The lighthouse was built in 1865 and decommissioned in the 1920s, but relit for a time in the 1980s after a campaign by yachtsmen.

Above: A modern office block dwarfs a 14th-century castle in Swansea. Wales's second city, Swansea was established as a port by the Normans. The original castle, built in 1106, was sacked by Welsh prince Owain Glyndwr and rebuilt in the 14th century. From 1306 Swansea had the Royal Charter to build and repair ships, a tradition continued into the 20th century.

Right: Swansea's maritime past is celebrated at the city's marina, which was created during the redevelopment of the docklands. Following the closure of the South Dock in 1969, work over several years led to the opening of a yacht marina in 1982. The Swansea Barrage, completed in 1992, extended the marina area at the mouth of the River Tawe.

Below: Swansea expanded to become a major industrial centre in
the 19th century through coal exports and the profits of anthracite
mining and the metal industry, and by the 1850s the city was supplying
60 per cent of the world's copper. Large parts of the docks have been
redeveloped, but the King's Dock remains in use for cargo operations.

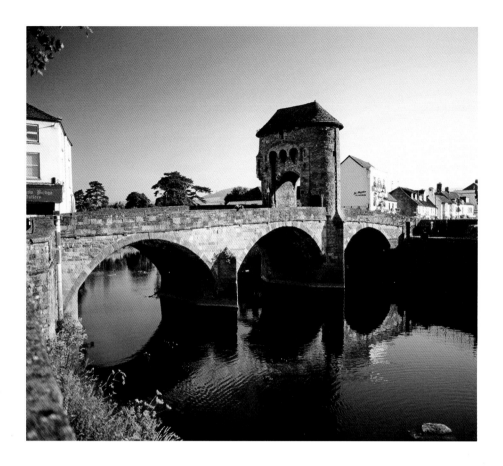

Opposite page: The Ashford Tunnel is a bottleneck on the Monmouthshire and Brecon Canal, just wide enough for one narrowboat at a time. In the days when craft were hauled by horses, men had to lie down across the boats and push them through the tunnel by walking their feet against the walls.

Right: A medieval fortified bridge crosses the River Monnow at Monmouth. The stone bridge was built around 1270, and the extraordinary gatehouse was added in the 14th century, perhaps as part of fortifications authorized by Edward I.

Below: Uprights reminiscent of an ancient stone circle on a hill between Ebbw Vale and Tredegar in Monmouthshire are in fact a memorial to Labour politician Aneurin Bevan. Born a miner's son in Tredegar, Bevan is remembered as a great orator and the architect of the National Health Service through his work as health minister in the 1945 Labour Government. He died in 1960, aged 62.

Right and below: Tintern Abbey, beautifully set on the west bank of the River Wye in Monmouthshire, is one of the most evocative monastic ruins in Britain. During the Romantic period it inspired painter JMW Turner as well as poet William Wordsworth, who wrote 'Lines composed a few miles above Tintern Abbey' in 1798. The abbey was founded for Cistercian monks by Walter de Clare, Lord of Chepstow, in 1131, then largely rebuilt in 1220–87. The cruciform church survives, though the remains are open to the skies.

Above: The 13th-century Caerphilly Castle is celebrated by architectural historians as Britain's first properly 'concentric' castle – one with twin protective walls, usually (as here) a lower outer wall overlooked by a taller and more formidable inner barrier. The impressive moat was reflooded as part of restorations around 1870.

Right: The transporter bridge across the River Usk at Newport, Gwent, was built in 1906 to designs by French engineer Ferdinand Arnodin. Between two towers 242ft (74m) high and 645ft (196.6 m) apart, a transporter platform carries goods across the river at a speed of up to 10ft (3m) a second. Widely recognized as a symbol of Newport, the bridge also carries a road and walkway.

Below: Standing at the end of the lake of Llyn Padarn, near Llanberis in Snowdonia, Dolbadarn Castle was used as a fortress of the Welsh princes until the early 15th century.

Right: In a commanding position atop a steep-sided rock, 200ft (60m) tall, Harlech Castle has the impregnable air of a fortress. Built in 1283-90, the castle has a concentric design, with inner and outer walls.

Overleaf: Mount Snowdon is reflected in the waters of Llynau Mymbyr, near Capel Curig. The lake, which lies in the valley of Dyffryn Mymbyr, is split in two by a delta roughly halfway along its length, from the northern shore. It is generally thought of as two lakes, and for this reason takes the plural form *Llynau* rather then the singular *llyn* or lake.

Above: The rising sun colours Mount Snowdon, as viewed from the arête or narrow ridge of Crib Gogh. Wales's tallest mountain, Snowdon – Yr Wyddfa in Welsh – rises 3,560ft (1,085m) above sea level. Its rocks date to the Ordovician period (490 to 443 million years ago) and have been substantially shaped by glaciation.

Right: A rack-and-pinion railway climbs 4.7 miles (7.6km) from Llanberis to the summit of Mount Snowdon. The railway was constructed in 1894–96, but the opening day at Easter 1896 was marred by a derailment in which a passenger died; after an inquiry the line reopened the following year. The station at the top of the line is just 68ft (20m) from the mountain's summit.

Below: The celebrated spiky rock formation near the summit of Glyder Fach in the Snowdonia National Park is called Castell y Gwynt ('The Castle of the Wind'). Glyder Fawr is visible in the background to the right.

Right: The path that climbs up to the Rhinogs in Snowdonia is called 'the Roman Steps'. The great rock slabs are in fact part of a medieval packhorse track, but the route was probably known to Roman soldiers.

Right: The handsome town of Brecon, in Powys, takes its name from Brychan, its Celtic governor in the 5th century. At the confluence of the rivers Usk, Honddu and Tarell, the settlement grew to prominence after the establishment of a castle in 1092 and a Benedictine monastery soon afterwards.

Below: The Craig Goch reservoir is one of four reservoirs in the Elan Valley, Powys, built in 1893–1904 as part of an ambitious scheme to supply water to Birmingham.

Opposite page: This cylindrical keep is the impressive remains of Tretower Castle in the Brecon Beacons National Park. The tower, which has three storeys and a basement, was built in the first half of the 13th century.

Right: Hardy Welsh mountain sheep graze on the grassy moors of the Brecon Beacons.

Below: The Brecon Beacons mountain range lies to the south of the market town of Brecon. The Beacons are so called from the ancient Welsh custom of lighting bonfire beacons to warn of English invasion.

Opposite page: The Black Mountains rise in the distance in this view from the bed of the River Usk. The mountains occupy the easternmost part of the Brecon Beacons National Park. The highest peak in the range is Waun Fach, which climbs to 2,661ft (811m). Others include Lord Hereford's Knob – a mere 2,264ft (690m) high.

Right: The early 18th-century bridge over the River Usk at Crickhowell, built in 1706, has a curious feature – there are 13 arches on one side and 12 on the other. This is because during widening on one side, two arches were replaced with one.

Below: At 2,907ft (886m), Pen y Fan is the principal peak in the Brecon Beacons. The obelisk in the foreground commemorates the tragic death of a five-year-old boy named Tommy Jones who became lost and died of exhaustion and hypothermia in 1900.

Below: On the Welsh border with England, the Offa's Dyke Path crosses Hay Bluff in the Black Mountains above Hay-on-Wye. The 177-mile (285km) route runs from Sedbury, near Chepstow to Prestatyn, largely following the great 8th-century defensive earthwork, built by Offa, ruler of the English kingdom of Mercia.

Overleaf: A typical landscape in the Brecon Beacons National Park combines grassy moorland and mature forestry plantations with green pasture down in the valleys, with the Talybont Reservoir providing a focal point. The area is also celebrated for the drama and beauty of its caves, waterfalls and lakes.

Index

Acknowledgments

The Automobile Association would like to thank the following photographers, companies and picture libraries for their assistance in the preparation of this book. Abbreviations for the picture credits are as follows – (t) top; (b) bottom; (c) centre; (l) left; (r) right; (AA) AA World Travel Library

2/3 AA/J Tims; 6b/7b AA/M Hamblin; 7tr AA/A Newey; 8tl AA/C Sawyer; 8cl AA/D W Robertson; 8bl Chris Howes/Wild Places Photography/Alamy; 9 AA/T Mackie; 10/11 AA/T Mackie; 12tr George Wheelhouse/Alamy; 12b photolibrary. com; 13 photolibrary.com; 14/15l AA/W Voysey; 15t AA/J Tims; 15b AA/J Tims; 16l Paul Airs/Alamy; 16r AA/R Duke; 17 AA/R Duke; 18/19 photolibrary.com; 20 AA/M Birkitt; 20r/21 AA/Vic Bates; 22tr AA/M Moody; 22bl AA/J Tims; 22br AA/M Moody; 23 AA/J Tims; 24 AA/T Mackie; 25t AA/M Moody; 25b AA/L Noble; 26tl AA/T Mackie; 26tr AA/T Mackie; 26b AA/M Birkitt; 27 AA/T Mackie; 28t Gavin Hellier/Alamy; 28b Kuttig - Travel/Alamy; 29 Eyebyte/ Alamy; 30t photolibrary.com; 30b AA/A Tryner; 31 Jon Arnold Images Ltd/ Alamy; 32 AA/A Burton; 33tl AA/J Hunt; 33b AA/A Burton; 34l AA/A Burton; 34l/35 AA/R Tennison; 36tl AA/A Mockford & N Bonetti; 36tr AA/R Coulam; 36b/37b AA/A Mockford & N Bonetti; 37tr AA/A Mockford & N Bonetti; 38tr AA/T Mackie; 38b AA/S Day; 39 AA/T Mackie; 40/41 AA/A Mockford & N Bonetti; 42/43 AA/T Mackie; 43tc AA/T Mackie; 43br AA/T Mackie; 44bl AA/T Mackie; 44r/45 AA/T Mackie; 46b/47b AA/T Mackie; 47tl AA/T Mackie; 47tr AA/T Mackie; 48bl AA/G Edwardes; 48r/49 AA/G Edwardes; 50tr AA/N Hicks; 50b AA/G Edwardes; 51 AA/A Burton; 52 AA/R Ireland; 53t AA/ AA; 53b AA/A Newey; 54t AA/A Newey; 54b AA/A Newey; 55 AA/A Newey; 56 AA/R Coulam; 56r/57 AA/R Coulam; 58 AA/N Setchfield; 58r/59l AA/M Birkitt; 59br AA/N Setchfield; 60t AA/S Day; 60b AA/S Day; 61t AA/M Moody; 61b AA/M Moody; 62c AA/D Hall; 62bl AA/S Day; 62r/63 AA/D Hall; 64b/65bl AA/W Voysey; 65tl AA/A Burton; 65br AA/A Burton; 66/67 AA/A Burton; 68bl AA/C Jones; 68br AA/C Jones; 69 AA/H Palmer; 70l AA/M Moody; 70br/71bl AA/M Moody; 71tl AA/M Moody; 71r photolibrary.com; 72tr Ed Rhodes/Alamy; 72b Greg Balfour Evans/Alamy; 72r/73 AA/V Bates; 74 AA/S McBride; 75b AA/A Burton; 76tr AA/A Newey; 76b AA/A Burton; 77 AA/N Setchfield; 78/79 AA/L Noble; 80tr Maurice Crooks/Alamy; 80b Manu/ Alamy; 81 AA/L Noble; 82 AA/D Clapp; 83tr AA/D Clapp; 83b AA/V Greaves; 84bl AA/S Day; 84r/85 AA/D Clapp; 86tr AA/J Tims; 86b photolibrary.com; 87 AA/J Tims; 88t Rod Edwards/Alamy; 88b AA/J Tims; 89t AA/J Tims; 89b AA/J Tims; 90l AA/J Tims; 90br AA/J Tims; 91bl AA/S Montgomery; 91r AA/S Montgomery; 92 AA/J Tims; 93 AA/J Tims; 94 AA/J Tims; 95tl AA/J Tims; 95b AA/J Tims; 96tr AA/J Tims; 96bl AA/N Setchfield; 96br AA/P Kenward; 97 AA/N Setchfield; 98tr photolibrary.com; 98b/99b photolibrary.com; 99tl Realimage/Alamy; 100 AA/D Clapp; 101 AA/D Clapp; 102/103l AA/T Mackie; 103br Richard Osbourne/Alamy; 104tl AA/T Mackie; 104b/105b AA/M Birkitt; 105tl AA/R Ireland; 105tr AA/T Mackie; 106tr Skyscan Photolibrary/Alamy; 106b photolibrary.com; 107 Colin Underhill/Alamy; 108/109l AA/R Coulam; 109br AA/R Coulam; 110r/111l AA/R Coulam; 111tr AA/R Coulam; 111cr AA/AA; 111br AA/J Hunt; 112l AA/J Tims; 112r/113l AA/AA; 113cr AA/J Tims; 113br photolibrary.com; 114tr/115tl AA/J Tims; 114b/115bl nobleIMAGES/Alamy; 115r Skyscan Photolibrary/Alamy; 116tl AA/J Tims; 116bl AA/J Tims; 116br AA/J Tims; 117 AA/J Tims; 118t/119tl AA/H Williams; 119r photolibrary.com; 120bl AA/M Morris; 120r/121 Skyscan Photolibrary/ Alamy; 122 David Bagnall/Alamy; 123t Carolyn Clarke/Alamy; 124/125l AA/J Tims; 125br AA/J Tims; 126bl AA/E Meacher; 126r/127 AA/C Jones; 128 AA/C Jones; 129tl AA/J Tims; 129bl AA/J Tims; 129br AA/J Tims; 130 AA/T Mackie; 131b photolibrary.com; 132tl AA/A Tryner; 132b AA/C Jones; 133 AA/C Jones; 134tc AA/T Mackie; 134tl AA/T Mackie; 134b/135b AA/T Mackie; 136bl AA/T Mackie; 136r/137 AA/T Mackie; 138bl AA/R Turpin; 138r AA/J Tims; 139tl Mike Booth/Alamy; 139b Robert Convery/Alamy; 140 AA/J Miller; 141t AA/J Miller; 141b AA/M Busselle; 142t AA/C Sawyer; 142b AA/ J Miller; 143 AA/J Miller; 144 AA/J Miller; 145t AA/L Noble; 145b AA/ J Miller; 146 AA/J Miller; 147 AA/J Miller; 148t AA/J Miller; 148bl AA/L Noble; 148br AA/ L Noble; 149 AA/L Noble; 150/151 AA/J Miller; 152/153l AA/R Coulam; 153br AA/R Coulam; 154 AA/C Jones; 155tl AA/C Jones; 155b AA/C Jones; 156bl AA/H Palmer; 156r/157 AA/C Jones; 158tl Craig Yates/Alamy; 158b AA/C Jones; 159 AA/C Jones; 160t AA/J Tims; 160b AA/M Moody; 161tl AA/M Moody; 161b AA/M Moody; 162/163 AA/M Moody; 164 AA/D Hall; 165bl AA/M Moody; 165br AA/C Jones; 166cl AA/D Clapp; 166bl AA/D Clapp; 166r/167 AA/D Clapp; 168tr AA/T Mackie; 168b/169bl AA/T Mackie; 169tl AA/T Mackie;

169r AA/M Kipling; 170b AA/D Clapp; 171 AA/D Clapp; 172bl AA/M Kipling; 172r/173 AA/T Mackie; 174bl Neale Clark/Robert Harding; 174br Cofiant/Alamy; 175tl photolibrary.com; 175b photolibrary.com; 176 AA/D Clapp; 177tr AA/D Clapp; 177b AA/D Clapp; 178/179 AA/M Hamblin; 180/181l AA/S Anderson; 181cl AA/S Anderson; 181b Mark Pink/Alamy; 182t David Robertson/Alamy; 182b Mike Rex/Alamy; 182r/183 AA/R Coulam; 184/185 Mark Pink/Alamy; 186bl AA/D W Robertson; 186r/187 AA/D W Robertson; 188b/189b AA/S Day; 189t AA/D W Robertson; 190/191l AA/D W Robertson; 191cr AA/D W Robertson; 191br AA/D W Robertson; 192/193l AA/M Alexander; 193c South West Images Scotland/ Alamy; 193bc David Lyons/Alamy; 194b/195bl Robert Harding Picture Library Ltd/Alamy; 195r AA/R Coulam; 196b Aidan Tompkins/Alamy; 197 D W Images Scotland/Alamy; 198bl AA/J Smith; 198r AA/J Smith; 199t AA/J Smith; 199b AA/J Smith; 200/201 photolibrary.com; 202tl photolibrary.com; 202b photolibrary.com; 203 photolibrary.com; 204 Graeme Peacock/Alamy; 205tr AzureRepublicPhotography/Alamy; 205b photolibrary.com; 206/207l AA/J Smith; 207tl AA/J Smith; 207b AA/J Smith; 208b Patrick Dieudonne/Robert Harding; 209 AA/S Whitehorne; 210/211 AA/J Henderson; 212tr AA/M Hamblin; 212b AA/S Whitehorne; 213t AA/M Hamblin; 213bl AA/J Smith; 214/215 AA/M Hamblin; 216/217l AA/J Smith; 217br AA/J Smith; 218tr AA/D Corrance; 218b AA/J Henderson; 219 AA/S Anderson; 220bl AA/S Whitehorne; 220r/221 AA/S Whitehorne; 222tr AA/K Blackwell; 222b AA/AA; 223tl AA/J Smith; 223tr AA/J Smith; 223b AA/J Smith; 224/225l Amanda Hall/Robert Harding; 226bl AA/J Smith; 226r/227 AA/J Smith; 228/229 AA/J Smith; 230 AA/S Whitehorne; 231tl AA/S Whitehorne; 231b AA/E Ellington; 232r/233 AA/S Whitehorne; 234bl AA/S Whitehorne; 234br AA/E Ellington; 235 AA/S Whitehorne; 236/237 Patrick Dieudonne/Robert Harding; 238tr National Geographic/Robert Harding; 238b National Geographic/Robert Harding; 239 David Robertson/Alamy; 240bl Juan Carlos Munoz/Robert Harding; 240br Patrick Dieudonne/Robert Harding; 241tl Michael knowles/Alamy; 241b Robert Harding/Alamy; 242tr AA/S Anderson; 242b/243b AA/S Anderson; 243tl AA/James Carney; 244 AA/D Forss; 244r/245 AA/ S Anderson; 246tr AA/S Whitehorne; 246bl AA/S Gibson; 246br Patrick Dieudonne/Robert Harding; 247 Tony Clerkson/Alamy; 248tr AA/S Whitehorne; 248b photolibrary. com; 249tl photolibrary.com; 249b John McKenna/Alamy; 250 AA/Steve Day; 250r/251 AA/S Whitehorne; 252/253 age fotostock/Robert Harding; 254 photolibrary.com; 254r/255 AA/S Day; 255tl PCL/Alamy; 255b David J Fleet/ Alamy; 256r AA/R Weir; 257 AA/S Day; 258 AA/S Whitehorne; 259 AA/S Whitehorne; 260/261 AA/H Williams; 262 DJ Downes / Alamy; 263t Photolibrary.com; 263b AA/ C Jones; 264/265 Alan Novelli/Alamy; 266c Andrew Jankunas/Alamy; 267 AA/C Jones; 268l AA/C Warren; 268r/269l AA/C Warren; 269r AA/C Warren; 270cl AA/C Warren; 270bl AA/C Warren; 270r/271 AA/C Warren; 272c AA/M Moody; 272b AA/M Moody; 273 Armand-Photo-Travel/Alamy; 274bl AA/C Warren; 274br/275b CW Images/ Alamy; 275t Pearl Bucknall/Robert Harding; 276l David Angel/Alamy; 276r/277 CW Images/Alamy; 280r The Photolibrary Wales/Alamy; 278b The Photolibrary Wales/Alamy; 279 Robert Garrigus/Alamy; 280 Jeff Morgan 01/Alamy; 281t AA/I Burgum; 281b Altimythpics/Alamy; 282 AA/R Duke; 283t AA/R Duke; 283b AA/R Duke; 284l AA/R Duke; 284r/285l AA/R Duke; 285br AA/R Duke; 286bl AA/H Williams; 286r/287 AA; 288 AA/ H Williams; 289 Adam Burton/Alamy; 289 AA/H Williams; 290 AA/M Moody; 291 Brilliant photography/ Alamy; 292tr AA/C Jones; 292br AA/C Jones; 293b AA; 294 AA; 295tl Graham Bell/Alamy; 295b AA/I Burgum; 296bl A Room With Views/ Alamy; 296r/297 AA/I Burgum; 298 Skyscan Photolibrary/Alamy; 299 SuperStock/Alamy; 300l AA/M Bauer; 300r/301 AA/M Bauer; 302/303 AA/S Watkins; 304tl James Osmond/Alamy; 304r/305 AA/S Lewis; 306 AA/S Lewis; 307 AA/S Lewis; 308tr AA/D Santillo; 308b AA/C Molyneux; 309 AA/D Santillo; 310tr AA/D Santillo; 310b AA/N Jenkins; 311 AA/C & A Molyneux; 312tr AA/D Santillo; 312b AA/N Jenkins; 313b AA/D Santillo; 314/315 AA/D Santillo.

Every effort has been made to trace the copyright holders, and we apologise in advance for any unintentional omissions or errors. We would be pleased to apply any corrections in a following edition of this publication.